To Patrick
[illegible]
[illegible]

A Six String History of America

Jay M. Pilzer

Grateful acknowledgement is given to authors, publishers and photographers for permission to reprint material. Every effort has been made to locate copyright owners of photographs and illustrations. In the case of any omissions, the publisher will be pleased to make suitable acknowledgments in future editions of this book.

Staunton, Virginia

(888) 521-1789

Visit us on the Internet at:

www.Americanhistorypress.com

ISBN 13: 978-1-939995-03-2

Library of Congress Control Number: 2014939544

July 2014

Manufactured in the United States of America on acid-free paper.

This book meets all ANSI standards for archival quality.

Table of Contents

Dedication

For Josh and Ethan, my two sons who have taken any talents I may have and multiplied them exponentially, and my late nephew Seth whose light was extinguished far too soon.

Foreword

There are numerous books on the market featuring the history of specific guitar manufacturers and their products. They often include photos of collectible instruments, identification guides for the various models, instruction books for players, and profiles of musicians and musical history, *A Six String History of America* takes quite a different approach.

Author Jay Pilzer, a former history professor, presents guitars, guitar makers, the guitar industry, and guitar players in a broad context, examining the role of guitars and guitar-centric music in American society. He looks at the role of demographics, technology, economics, social history, race, and popular culture from the early 1800s to the present time. With the exception of classical and flamenco guitars, virtually all types of guitars in common use today and much of the music played on them evolved in the United States. Over the past two centuries the instruments, the music, and their role in American society have undergone a dramatic transformation, which Jay has presented very engagingly in a comprehensive historical context.

Jay is especially well qualified to offer such a presentation since he is not only a highly-educated historian and careful researcher, but also a player and songwriter. He has been buying, selling, and trading guitars as a guitar dealer for over twenty years, first as a sideline supplementing his teaching income, and, since his retirement as a history professor, as the source of his primary income. Jay's presentation combines the focus of a carefully trained academic researcher with many years of hands-on direct personal experience with guitars, music, and musicians.

I feel fortunate to be able to count Jay as a friend. In our numerous, almost daily, conversations over the years we have both learned a great deal from each other. On many occasions our discussions and intellectual debates have resulted in changing long-held opinions, which both of us find very refreshing. I recommend *A Six String History of America* as an informative, engaging, and thought-provoking book. I expect it to appeal to guitar players, dealers, collectors, and anyone interested in the role of guitars and music in American culture.

George Gruhn
Gruhn Guitars
Nashville, Tennessee

Introduction and Acknowledgments

There is no single product that has reflected the spread of American culture as much as the guitar. Although this instrument did not originate in North America, it is there that it has found its most popular expression. Its use has spread until it can be found virtually everywhere, playing music that was specifically composed for it and, in some cases, being adopted into the music of cultures where the instrument was previously unknown.

America's greatest cultural exports are, I believe, blues, jazz, country, and, most significantly, rock and roll. The latter could not have developed anywhere except the United States, since it originated from a combination of African rhythms, the storytelling and ballads of England, and a variety of other local forms. "The blues...," according to Muddy Waters, "...had a baby and they called it rock 'n roll." The instrument that has been most common to all of these styles has been the guitar.

What makes this particular instrument so popular? There are a variety of reasons. The guitar has been called a handheld orchestra. It has a wide range of tones and can accommodate a similarly expansive variety of musical styles. It is also a perfect selection to accompany the human voice. These elements make it useful and beautiful. I bought my first guitar more than fifty years ago and love them as much today as I did back then.

This is a book of synthesis. It is neither an exhaustive look at American history nor a comprehensive history of American music. Instead, it is a series of essays that look at some important and fascinating aspects of American history, guitars, the guitar business, and the music played on them. Neither American popular music nor guitars exist in a vacuum. Both exist in and are part of the broader context of history.

While there is some continuity among chapters and they are written roughly in chronological order, I have sought to make each chapter basically stand alone. Thus, if readers are only interested in two or three subjects they can read the appropriate chapters. To that end, I have mentioned some issues briefly in one chapter that may have a more expansive treatment in a latter one.

Making and selling guitars is exactly like manufacturing and selling other products until it is not—and then it is dramatically different. Raw materials, labor, tools, and financial resources come into play, just as they do for refrigerators, clocks, televisions, or cars. Guitars, however, have several distinguishing characteristics that make the industry unique. The most significant of these to my mind, are: someone must learn to play them if they are to be useful, they are traditionally made of wood (which adds all manner of complexity to the process of both construction and distribution), and their evaluation can often be very subjective. Companies that have failed to recognize these unique qualities of the guitar have by and large failed.

I have read many times that a book is never written alone. I never understood exactly what that meant until I started writing. There have been a variety of people who have been very generous with their time and knowledge during the process. George Gruhn, a great friend, expert on guitars, and owner of Gruhn Guitars in Nashville, has been essential. He has read every word and offered expansive critiques of my work along the way. While the errors or omissions are my own, George played an important role in expanding my vision and lessening my mistakes. Thank you George.

The following people have also been very generous with their time and expertise: Bruce Bolen (jazz player and former executive at both Gibson and Fender), Susan Carson (a fine musician and former Fender rep with a keen sense of that company's history), Tim Shaw (both Gibson and Fender have used his talents), Dan Smith (who joined Fender with the late Bill Schultz and was instrumental in the resurrection of the brand), Lindy Fralin (expert pickup designer and manufacturer), Mark French (engineering professor and consultant on guitar design), Dick Boak (many years with Martin in various positions and a walking history of the company), Michael Dickenson (Martin's wood buyer; also in charge of the museum), Albert Germick (who performs testing at Martin), Grieg Hutton (who has done remarkable work in Martin's documents), Augie Lye (the inventor of the Tonerite), the late Jim Gurley (president of Ovation Guitars), Tom Holmes (pickup guru), Ashvin Coomar (president of Rainsong Guitars), Walter Carter (author of many excellent books about guitar history), Brenda Colladay (who may know more about the history of country music than anyone on the planet), Brian Majeski (editor of *The Music Trades* magazine), Matt McPherson (president of McPherson Guitars), Roger Siminoff (long time guitar designer and builder), Gill Hembree (editor of *The Official Vintage Guitar Price Guide*), Ned Steinberger (inventor and instrument designer), Paul Reed Smith, (OK—this one should be obvious), Jeanne Nooney (of PRS Guitars), Hank Sable (whose insightful question one day brought focus to this book), Darryl Hattenhauer (an English professor and fellow guitar lover), Jay McDowell (a good friend and great musician who helped me explore some of these themes over lunch), Dan Fiorentino (who directs the NAMM oral history project), Mason William (musician, writer, and activist), and David Kane (publisher and editor of this book). Your patience and devotion to this project is greatly appreciated, and I thank you all.

In addition to George Gruhn I was blessed with several other readers who viewed this work from their own unique perspectives. My sister, Deanna Miller, taught history for many years, and her keen analysis has been of immeasurable importance. She has made it clear when I have said too little or too much on any subject or when a topic needed clarification.

Richard Moore, a retired English professor, has similarly been helpful in pointing out deficiencies and verbosity. In addition, he certainly knows his way around a comma. His detailed and articulate comments have made this book more readable and improved clarification on several subjects.

I was very lucky to have these well-informed readers who are not immersed in guitar culture. Their perspectives have, I hope, allowed me to write a book that will please two broad categories of reader: those interested in an overall view of the guitar and those who would find the central theme of guitars an interesting approach to some issues of the American past.

I also want to acknowledge the role of Renée White from the Tennessee State Museum. The germ of this book was planted while I was working on a committee to put together an exhibit on American guitars. Throughout this process I began to ask myself questions about the relationship of guitars to larger themes in the American past. This book is a result of that process.

This book has been a joy to write. It has combined my passion for guitars with my training as a historian. I can only hope that you find these essays interesting, illuminating, and even, dare I say, entertaining.

Jay Pilzer
Nashville Tennessee
July 2014

CHAPTER ONE

One Nation One Brand

The United States changed a great deal during the nineteenth century. Its economy transformed from localized to regional, and finally to a national level. It went from a nation that lived primarily on the East Coast to one that incorporated and settled the western reaches of an ever-expanding United States. The creation of national brands became possible only when transportation and communications would allow it. Over time this took place in many industries and with many commodities.

One guitar company exists today that was a prime player during the time period described above. That company, of course, is Martin Guitars. First established in New York City in 1833, this Nazareth, Pennsylvania company has established itself over its long life span as one of the world's premier guitar makers. It has also been responsible for the vast amount of innovation and popularization of the guitar.

There were many great debates during the founding years of the United States. One of the most significant of these was between the proponents of an exclusively agricultural country, led by Thomas Jefferson, and the followers of Alexander Hamilton, who believed that the United States should have a mixed economy that supported agriculture, manufacturing, and commerce. Heavy industry and the use of power equipment in large factories would come into its own after the Civil War. But manufacturing was really pre-industrial, and it consisted of small workshops making products out of raw materials. That is the very definition of the Martin guitar company, particularly in the years after it moved from New York to Pennsylvania in 1839.

When Christian Frederick Martin moved to the United States from his native Germany and started his company in New York, he had conveniently established himself in the center of American business, in general, and the instrument business in particular. Martin built and repaired guitars, sold European brands, and carried a wide range of instruments and the accessories that went with them. Flutes, violins and related string instruments, as well as other non-guitar items, formed a major part of his business. That would soon change in Pennsylvania.

After originating in Spain, the guitar had become a very fashionable instrument in Europe and makers in France, England, Germany, and Spain

C.F. Martin

had become quite adept at their work. There were, however, no American guitars that were being commercially produced when Martin opened for business.

C. F. Martin would alter all of that. When he closed his New York operation and moved to Pennsylvania he changed his focus from being a general music store to becoming an exclusive maker of guitars. He also left much of the distribution and sales to others. The majority of Martin's early production went to one New York wholesaler who would go on to distribute Martin guitars to an ever-widening American market.

Martin's guitars changed significantly through the years. While in New York, Martin had offered tuner and headstock options: six-on-a-side Stauffer style geared tuners, three-on-a-side peg tuners, and three-on-a-side geared tuners with a slotted headstock. In Nazareth the Stauffer headstock was soon replaced by the now iconic squared off headstock. Two versions were made available: a solid headstock with three-on-a-side peg tuners and the slotted three-on-a-side headstock with geared tuners.

Most significant, however, was Martin's dramatic change in bracing the guitar soundboard or top. Herein lays the cornerstone of Martin Guitars. Guitars of this era were all played with gut strings and their tops were braced with lateral braces that ran from one side of the guitar straight across to the other. Martin changed this to an "X" style bracing, where the main braces make an "X" near the sound hole. While today we associate the "X" type brace with steel-string guitars, this was not the case at this design's inception. Martin found that his method of bracing provided extra strength and also improved the tone of his instruments. Although some early examples exist from the 1840s, the "X" brace really became established as a Martin standard during the next decade.

In Europe the "fan" bracing system was also under development. This was perfected by Spanish luthier Antonio Torres in the 1850s and has become the standard for classical guitars today. It was not popularized in the United States until the twentieth century. In the nineteenth century the "X" braced Martin was, if not dominant in sheer numbers sold, considered to be the best example of American guitars.

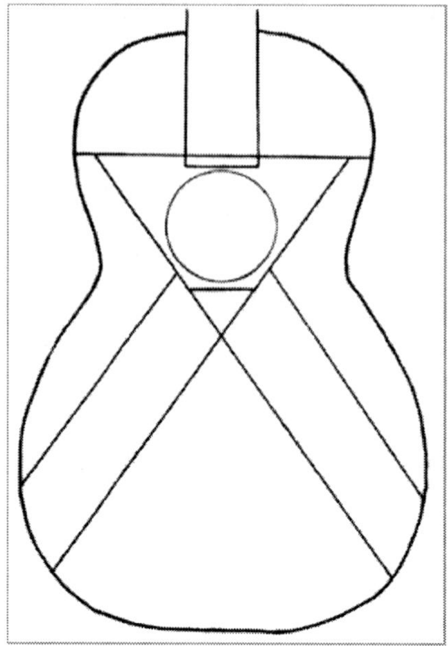

Early Martin "X" brace pattern

The guitar in the nineteenth century was increasing in popularity as both an instrument in its own right and as an instrument to accompany the voice. Its range of tones was regarded as a perfect complement to singing. Men and women played guitars, but the latter appear to have been the greater market. Playing an instrument was a basic skill for upper class young women, and the guitar soon gained popularity among them. This trend was aided by the demographic increase in the ranks of middle and upper class women as the United States moved into commerce and manufacturing. This produced a more dynamic economy that in turn produced more wealth. Thus some of the largest buyers of guitars were schools for young woman.

The story of Martin's growth is not only a tale of one guitar manufacturer. It also chronicles the story of a transportation revolution that allowed the creation of a national distribution system that, along with skilled manufacturing and design, would establish C. F. Martin & Company as America's premier guitar brand.

When most of the states of our union were located on the coast, the majority of transportation routes ran up and down the Atlantic seaboard, throughout the Chesapeake Bay, or on rivers that, east of the Appalachians, are primarily oriented north-south. As land prices continued to rise in the east, settlers pushed further west, an area then defined as the terrain between the Appalachian Mountains and the Mississippi River. For these western territories to become part of the United States there had to be communication and transportation, because without those basic necessities in place, those lands would become isolated settlements.

c.1834 Martin Stauffer style

There were several attempts to join the east and west in the early part of the nineteenth century. Many explorers looked for a river that would penetrate the interior, but none was found. A turnpike boom started in 1794 and lasted for twenty years. The primary function of these private for-profit roads, however, was to link eastern cities.

The most significant early pathway west was the National Road, which was started in 1811 and not completed until 1852. Starting in Cumberland, Maryland it spanned for 591 miles all the way to Vandalia, Illinois. This project, funded by federal and state governments, was the best available route in its day, but it did have its drawbacks. It was difficult to maintain, and the transportation of people and goods in wagons pulled by oxen and horses was laborious, limiting, and expensive.

River traffic was a significant means to travel into the interior but for all intents and purposes it was one way only—north to south. A flatboat would be built upriver, loaded with people and goods, floated downriver to a port, and then disassembled and sold for either firewood or building material. The trip upriver would be by foot or horseback, since it was too difficult to go against the current. Nothing but the smallest and lightest of manufactured items could make that trip.

The steamboat, which became commercially viable in 1807, changed all of that. It now made it possible for goods to travel both ways on American rivers. By 1830 there were more than two hundred steam vessels on the Mississippi, and for the first time settlers in America's interior could fully become a functioning part of the national economy.

A second innovation also had its origins in water transportation. This was the great canal boom that followed the opening of New York's Erie Canal in 1827. This marvel of engineering connected the Hudson River with the Great Lakes, thus joining the thriving American East Coast ports with the interior of the country. When completed the canal reduced the transit time from New York City to Buffalo from twenty days to six days. The cost of moving a ton of freight over that same distance decreased from one hundred dollars to five dollars. The northern part of the nation's West was now connected to the great business centers of the East and through them to European markets. Following the great success of the Erie Canal other states built similar systems. However, canals were laborious and costly undertakings. And they were limited in the sense that they could only connect already-existing waterways.

A few decades later railroads were first introduced in the United States. In 1832 the B&O, the nation's first railroad, had seventy-three miles of track. By 1840 the United States had more railroad companies, and they had lain over 3,000 miles of track, and by 1860 this number had increased to

River steamboat c.1850

The Erie Canal

over 30,000 miles. Nearly three-quarters of this was in the northern United States. Although railroads were difficult and expensive to build, they were far more cost effective and time-saving than canals, and they had less physical limitations.

Early railways were not part of a coordinated system. The private companies that owned them often used different gauges of track to insure that some other company's trains could not run on their rails. While this was a clever attempt to keep a monopoly on local transport, it soon became apparent that an amalgamated system was necessary. Standard gauges of track were soon established and a uniform railway system was developed.

By 1850 Martin guitars were being distributed in an ever-widening area. But the improvement in transportation was not the primary reason that Martin guitars gained wider distribution. The main cause was that Martin established a reputation for beautiful-looking guitars and, more important to musicians, guitars with superior tone. At the New York Crystal Palace exhibition in 1853 Martin was awarded a bronze medal in the musical instrument category. There were other guitar makers present and some had beautiful guitars. But Martin overshadowed them because theirs were the best sounding, most well-constructed, and better playing guitars at the exhibition.

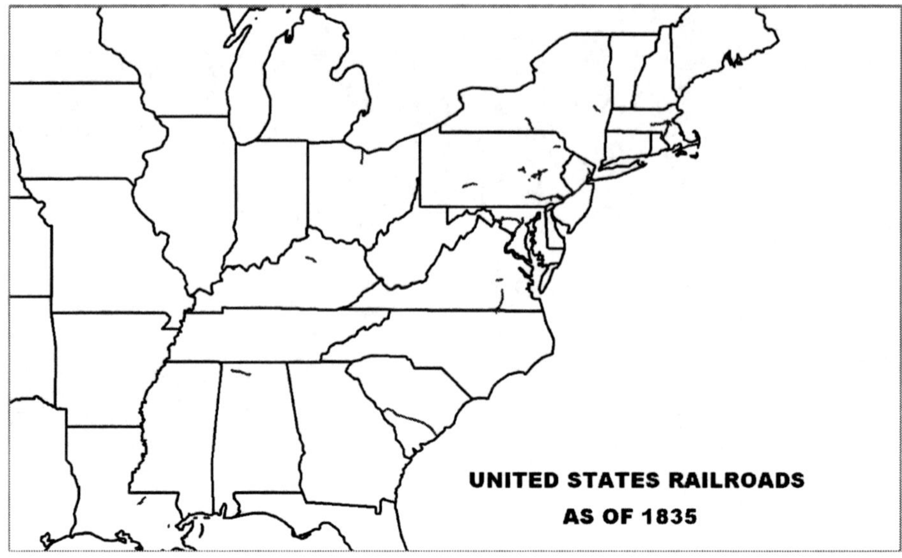

U.S. Railroad trackage 1835

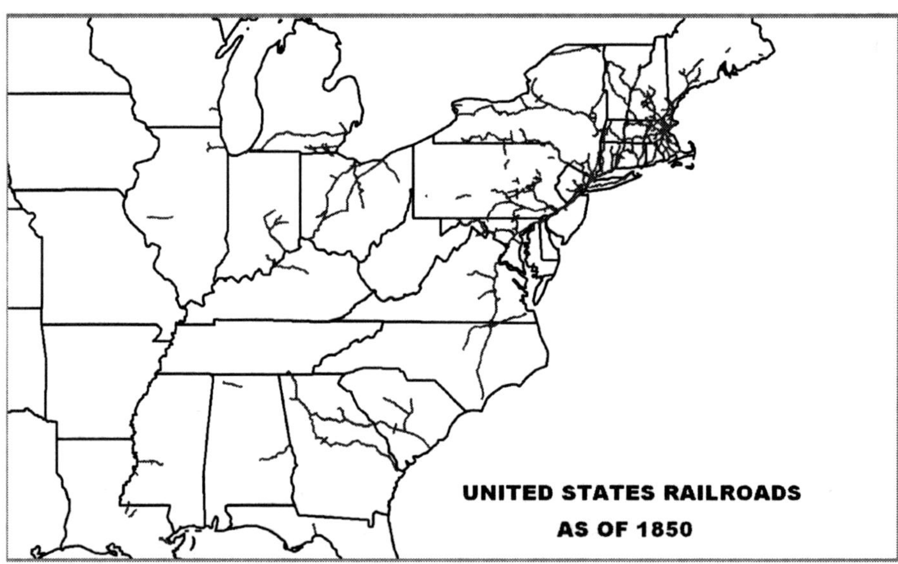

U.S. Railroad trackage 1850

The combination of Martin quality with improved distribution allowed C. F. Martin to become the premier brand of guitars in antebellum America. The range of the company's sales was truly remarkable. Martins were shipped as far west as Chicago, Nashville, and Memphis. They were sold in the Deep South states of Louisiana, Mississippi, and, Alabama. The northern range spread to Boston, Canada and as far west as Cleveland, Ohio. Without the expansion of transportation all commerce—guitars included—was essentially local, but with a national transportation system in place business now thrived.

Widening distribution led to an increase in production to keep up with demand. This caused Martin to create a standardized system to designate size and ornamentation that still exists to this day. By the middle of the 1850s Martin had seven sizes—5, 4, 3, 2 ½, 2, 1, and 0—with the last being the largest. Prior to this time models were named after various artists or were essentially "one-offs" that were made to the specifications requested by the buyer. That system did not have the uniformity that the company needed to fulfill their increase in orders. Once the new system was in place, it enabled the company's workers to speed up production and fulfill demands for their products on a timely basis.

As mentioned, Martin was not alone in American guitar building prior to the Civil War. The same transportation system that allowed Martin to become a national brand led other manufacturers to enter the market. But widening distribution was only one factor that drew others to the guitar industry. The other key factor was an increasing interest in guitars and other musical instruments.

Several New York music stores were major distributors for musical instruments. Today we would call these people wholesalers. They, when combined with the regular customers of Martin, were placing ever-increasing orders that Martin was unable to fill. In some cases retailers and wholesalers would simply tell the company to send whatever they had in stock. In particular it was the less expensive instruments that were in high demand.

Martin could not fulfill this surge of orders. While they were using some power equipment such as steam-powered saws, they were still, in essence, a small manufacturer that had not made the shift to the large-scale industry that would become the hallmark of American manufacturing after the Civil War. The Ashborn guitar manufacturing company of Connecticut took advantage of Martin's plight, and quickly stepped in as a competitor. While Martin was making 250 guitars a year, Ashborn would routinely make 70 *per month* and sometimes as many as one hundred.

Why was Ashborn able to speed up production? Ashborn, like Martin, was effectively a workshop. They were, however, significantly larger in terms of employee numbers and space than Martin, and they utilized more power equipment. Another advantage was that they made their own metal tuning machines. In addition, all of their guitars were the same size and had similar construction, and were only differentiated by materials used and appointments. When combined, these improvements allowed for faster production at a lower cost.

In comparison, Ashborn production numbers were significantly higher than Martin, but the figures were very small compared to the quantities the industry would see by the late nineteenth and early twentieth centuries.

Ashborn guitars were of high quality, and they sold well. They did not, however, compare with the quality of their Pennsylvania rival. In particular, the neck joint was based on a particularly poor design. Thus, over the years, their instruments have not lasted as long as Martins.

Both Martin and Ashborn used what was called the American System of manufacturing. This was an intermediate step between the single craftsmen era and industrial mass production. Prior to the American System, a shop would consist of one or two craftsmen who would make all of the parts for the finished product. Guns, for example, were made by gunsmiths who crafted all the guns' components in their own shop. Each finished product was then an individual and nearly unique item, a true "one-off."

The American System modified this method. Multiple craftsmen would make various parts, stocks, barrels, trigger assemblies, hammers, and other necessary parts which would be then be assembled to become the completed product. This system, the precursor to Henry Ford's moving assembly line, allowed for more rapid production. It also demanded standardization of parts and the regulation of completed products.

This was the system employed by both Martin and Ashborn. By 1850 Martin had seven employees. Each specialized in one or two areas of production. Their various parts were then assembled into the complete guitar which was then given its finishing touches. C. F. himself oversaw the entire process, and as a result Martin quality was very consistent.

This period was not the last time that Martin would be confronted with issues between increasing production and preserving quality. The 1960s and '70s would see this recur in a much more dramatic fashion for Martin and every other American guitar manufacturer. In the 1990s and in the early part of the twenty-first century production would again increase drastically with a concurrent pressure to maintain quality.

Martin was part of a larger economic system that had far reaching political consequences. The vast majority of American manufactured goods came out of the northern states while the South provided raw materials and markets. At the onset of the Civil War New York alone produced ten times the manufactured goods of the entire South combined. At this time there were no significant guitar makers in the southern United States.

The result of this variability in manufacturing between these two regions was a major factor in the coming and, of course, the outcome of the Civil War in the United States between 1861 and 1865. By 1860 the South had lost its economic and political dominance of the nation, and many Southerners felt that there was a Northern plot to make the South an "economic colony" of the North. The actuality had much more to do with the flow of change than any active plan. The South was wedded economically, socially, and politically to an antiquated system based on raw materials coupled with slave labor. Wealth was concentrated in very few hands. So while some owners of major cotton plantations had great wealth, the region as a whole could not compete with the more varied economy of the northern states. Simply put, in an exchange of goods between raw materials and manufactured goods the region that is selling the latter will suck money out of the former.

The period from 1820 to 1860 also saw the introduction of new methods of long distance payment. A Martin vendor in Nashville, for example, could issue Martin a letter of credit in payment that could be redeemed at a New York or Philadelphia bank. This ability to transfer funds with confidence

The old North Street Martin factory today

and safety was another essential ingredient in the emergence of a national economy.

The combination of expanding transportation, communication, and financial systems made it possible for Martin to become a national guitar brand. From Nazareth, Pennsylvania, C.F. Martin created a company that began as a regional one and became a national one, and today the Martin guitar brand is a well-known player in the global economy.

CHAPTER TWO

Jimi Hendrix's Coal-Fired Stratocaster

In 1969 Jimi Hendrix climbed up on the stage at Woodstock, played his highly distorted version of The Star-Spangled Banner, and caused a sensation heard around the world. This was a seminal moment in American musical history. It was loud and rebellious, and it took the guitar to places it had never been before. Jimi played a Fender Stratocaster that day and, if it were not for an odd combination of events, his guitar of choice may never have existed. That Strat came into existence through a long series of national and international events that had started nearly a century before Woodstock.

It all began in Texas, the home of guitar slingers from Charlie Christian to Stevie Ray Vaughan, which seems an appropriate place to start since this is, after all, a story about guitars. The Texas rebellion against the Mexican government led to the annexation of Texas by the United States in 1845. The Mexican government had previously stated that such an annexation would be viewed as an act of war. As a result the United States and Mexico engaged in a conflict between 1846 and 1848 that would forever change the United States and, coincidentally, American music and guitars.

With the 1848 Treaty of Guadalupe Hidalgo that ended the Mexican War, the United States took possession of California. That land had been in American sights for several years, and with the Mexican war possession of California had become a reality. Its population would soon swell with the massive influx of the "'49ers" after gold was discovered there.

With its territory now bordered by two oceans, the United States was at the center of the world. It enjoyed vast natural resources, an ever-increasing pool of labor, and an embrace of industry. The country could now follow a path

Jimi Hendrix

that would move it from the edge of power to the center. American goods and ideas would soon travel the world, and the products of the world would move to America across the same two oceans.

Then, as now, China and Japan offered huge markets for American goods. Additionally, Protestant missionaries were expanding their activities in Asia. This combination of trade and missionary activity gave the United

States the responsibility of protecting its citizens in these far-flung corners of the earth.

By the late part of the nineteenth century the United States had a new definition of Manifest Destiny—a nearly divine mandate. The numbers from the census of 1890 had declared that the American frontier was gone. There was simply no locale in the mainland United States that had a population density low enough to be considered *frontier*. The United States, some historians believe, had been culturally, economically, and politically driven by expansionism. That which had once been contained within the North American continent would now translate into a desire for expansion overseas.

This was a new idea. The United States was no longer considered a mere footnote to European economies. The country had rapidly evolved to becoming one of the most powerful industrial states on the planet, driven by a combination of economic yearnings, a search for Protestant converts and a desire among some capitalists to take its rightful place as a major international player. In response, the United States developed the two-ocean navy required to protect its trade routes and the citizens that used them.

A modern navy now became an important priority for the United States—a navy propelled by steam. While steamships offer great advantages over sailing ships, they do have one great drawback—they require a constant supply of fuel. That is not a great problem when you're dealing with river travel or coastal trade, but it is a far different story when you're trying to cross vast oceans. This predicament was partially solved by an increase in efficiency in steam engines. Although this worked out the challenges involved with crossing the Atlantic, even the most efficient engines could not cross the wider Pacific Ocean without intermediate coaling stations. A ship that carried enough fuel to make it across the Pacific would have little if any room for cargo, thus defeating its use for trade.

That fact drove the United States toward some of its first colonial adventures. The country secured fueling rights in Samoa, and shortly thereafter began a relationship with Hawaii. It is this relationship that leads us on the long, winding, and quite muddy road to Woodstock. In the last years of the nineteenth century American planters and missionaries had come to dominate Hawaiian economics and politics. Several treaties and trade agreements had been made and abandoned.

The Spanish-American War, at the dawn of the twentieth century (1898-1901), was America's debut as a full-fledged participant in international politics and warfare. While the conflict began over the Spanish colony of Cuba, Spain also held the Philippines, and when the Treaty of Paris was signed at the war's conclusion the United States was ceded control of the Philippine islands. The United States had been a Pacific power, but now it had possessions in Asia, thousands of miles from its own coast.

At the same time we solidified our relationship with Hawaii. An American-sponsored coup, combined with political maneuvering, deposed the last Hawaiian queen, and the United States formally annexed Hawaii in 1898. The nation now had the perfect geographic midpoint to support both commercial and military Pacific fleets, and in the process had planted the musical seed from which the solid body electric guitar would grow.

Musically, in 1900, the United States was in the firm grip of the mandolin age. Mandolin clubs and mandolin orchestras dominated popular music. Their sound was new to American ears and had risen to compete with the banjo, an instrument which had been popular since the 1840s. The mandolin had been imported with the wave of immigration from Italy and other parts of Europe, so most of the mandolin music being played had a mixture of European and American origins. The mandolin was supplemented with the mandola, the mandocello, and the mandolin bass in order to approximate a full orchestral sound.

But the mandolin phenomenon was about to be challenged. In January 1912 the Hawaiian-themed show *Bird of Paradise* opened on Broadway. It soon had to relocate to a larger theater to accommodate the swelling crowds of enthusiastic fans. In 1915 the Panama Pacific International Exposition opened in San Francisco. Hawaiian music was an integral part of the displays where Hawaiian women danced the hula in their grass skirts. Many Americans became captivated and enthralled by the flowing sounds of this exotic music.

The United States' decisive role in World War I accelerated America's dominance in international politics, economics, and culture. While our entry

Mandolin Orchestra

into the war in 1917 was a delayed one, since the conflict had begun in 1914, our presence was critical to the Allied victory.

Hawaiian exotica

Americans marched off to war with idealism and a song. They returned with a cynicism borne of their struggle in the trenches of Western Europe. This cynicism was heightened by the activities of Great Britain, France, and Italy at the Peace Conference of 1919 after the Allied victory. Here, the victorious powers seemed to revert to their colonial ambitions that preceded the war. France, in particular, wanted revenge on Germany, and wished to impose crippling sanctions that would guarantee that they would never again have to fear an invasion from that country. Earlier idealism had been replaced by the cold realities of war and international politics.

At home the United States faced an almost schizophrenic duality. On one hand Americans had become invested as a world power. Men had marched off to war from cities and towns across the country and had come home forever changed. But many Americans were disillusioned. Some believed that their idealistic struggle had become business as usual for the European powers. There was also a fear that membership in the proposed League of Nations, the short-lived predecessor of the United Nations, would drag the United States into European affairs beyond what was in the nation's best interest. In short, many wanted to return to a simpler time. As a consequence, the nation rejected membership in the League.

There were other popular movements that gave evidence of American desires to retreat into a world that had once been. New restrictions were placed on immigration, the Ku Klux Klan emerged as a powerful force against change, and Prohibition would attempt to restore an American morality that had perhaps never existed.

Other groups of Americans fully embraced change. This was reflected in dress, sexual behavior, and music. America had emerged as a global power with interests in Asia, the Caribbean, and other parts of the world, but, more importantly to our story, Americans had been exposed to broad cultural influences that expanded their musical tastes. Different trends in music emerged after the war and competed for attention in popular culture. These included the tango, blues, jazz, big bands, and other types that were exciting, new, and exotic to American ears. As a result, the mandolin had faded from popularity by the early 1920s.

Hawaiian music again took the stage. The fascination with this type of music that had begun before the war had rapidly accelerated afterwards as more Americans had been exposed to a broader world. This trend had a broad influence on American music, particularly in the realm of guitars and guitar compositions.

The Portuguese first introduced the guitar to Hawaii. Soon indigenous Hawaiians had adapted the instrument to create a variety of musical styles. One of these incorporated musical passages that flowed from note to note. Another was played on the fretted ukulele, an instrument based on the guitar family. Both types of Hawaiian music swept across America, and the ukulele

The DeLano
Hawaiian Steel Guitar and Ukulele Sextette of Los Angeles

C. S. DeLANO, *Director*
Piano, MRS. C. S. DeLANO *Soprano*, EVANGELINE CARROLL
Readings, MISSES H. TOBIAS *and* E. CARROLL
Steel Guitar and Ukulele:
MISSES H. TOBIAS, E. CARROLL, H. DeLANO, B. DeLANO, MESSRS R. BURGOIN *and* C. S. DeLANO

Hawaiian group

in particular became a huge seller among fretted instrument manufacturers who offered a range of these instruments. C. F. Martin, for example, produced about 10,000 ukes in 1925.

The other instrument essential for Hawaiian music was the Hawaiian guitar. When played with a bar slid down the strings to produce the sweeping pitches of the islands, a new sound emerged that was produced when the player's fingers plucked the strings with one hand while sliding the bar with the other. This melodic style of Hawaiian guitar music could not be played on a fretted guitar. It required the broad movement between notes that only a slide guitar could make.

This new music brought to mind warm beaches, swaying palm trees, and the swaying hips of young island girls in grass skirts. It was also a music that could, as contemporary advertisements claimed, be learned easily. In a matter of weeks one could become the hit of the party—a virtual Hawaiian guitar god.

Resonator Guitars—some came with Hawaiian scenes engraved or painted

At first, regular Spanish style guitars (those which we now call standard guitars), were modified to play Hawaiian music. Raised nuts were used to increase the distance of the strings from the fretboard so that the slide could be easily manipulated without the interference of the frets. These Hawaiian style guitars lay flat on the player's lap or in front on a stand. Later, employing different shapes and features, companies like Martin, Lyon and Healy, Knutsen, Weissenborn, and Gibson began to make guitars specifically for the Hawaiian music market.

As audience sizes increased and guitars came into wider use, manufacturers were in search of a way to make their instruments louder. In response, both Martin and Gibson made larger flat top guitars. The first Martin Dreadnought, made for the Ditson Company in 1916, was geared toward Hawaiian music. The competition between Gibson and Epiphone for the largest archtop became a running battle. Perhaps the most radical non-electric innovation was that of the Dopyera Brothers who, along with George Beauchamp, introduced the first resonator instruments. These had thin metal speaker-style cones that produced increased volume without any electronic aid. Then, as now, these guitars were seen as well suited for slide work. Both blues and Hawaiian music adopted these new instruments.

George Beauchamp

Another alternative for volume was the electronic pickup and amplifier combination. There had been earlier attempts to produce an electronic amplification system for guitars. These efforts did not amplify the strings themselves, but rather the vibrations made by the bridge.

George Beauchamp, working with Adolph Rickenbacker, created the first electro-magnetic pickup in 1931. The two men formed the Ro-Pat-In Corporation which would later become Rickenbacker. Beauchamp's pickup, easily identified by the large "horse shoe" magnet used to create the magnetic field, initiated a process that changed both guitars and the music made with them. Early experiments with hollow body guitars fitted with pickups had proved unsatisfactory. Beauchamp and others believed that the acoustic qualities of an instrument, the resonances and overtones so sought after before amplification, were an impediment to a clear amplified sound.

The new pickup was mounted on a cast aluminum body that was hollow to save weight. Since it lacked sound holes, it functioned as a solid body. The "Electro Hawaiian Guitar," often called "the frying pan" because of its round body with a neck extending like a long handle, was the first successful solid body electric guitar. The slightly bewildered patent office did not know whether to call it a musical instrument or an "electrical device." The inventors sent noted Hawaiian guitarist Sol Hoopii to Washington to play it and show that the invention worked.

The basic design of this pickup, and nearly every magnetic pickup since, was based on a magnetic field that responded to the vibration of the strings. This very weak electronic impulse was sent via a cord to an amplifier which would (wait for it) amplify the signal, and then send it out through a speaker. A new sound was born which would soon have many applications.

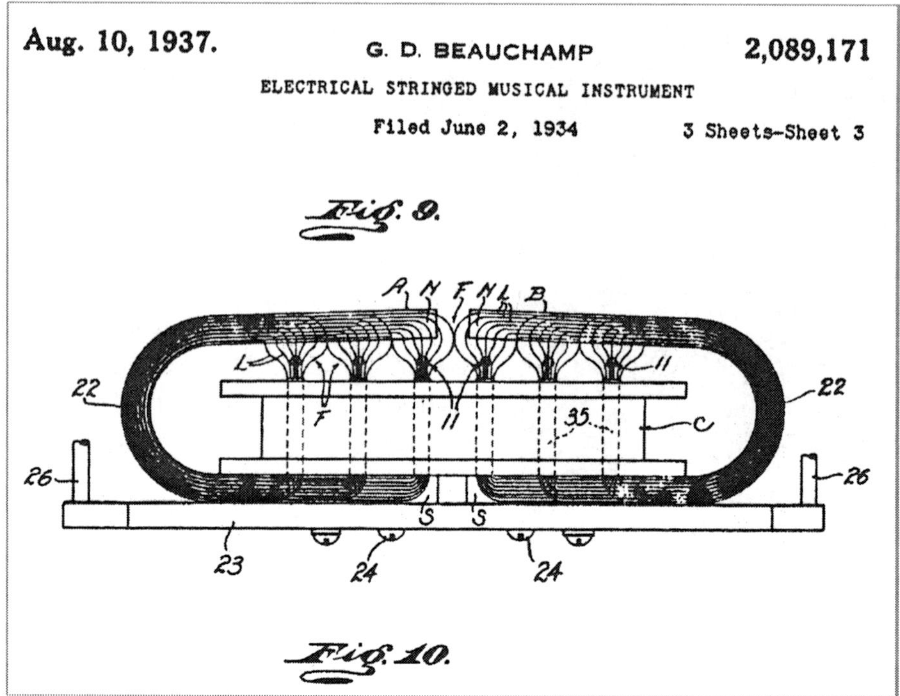

Beauchamp's horseshoe pickup design

The National Guitar Company, Vivi-Tone, and Rickenbacker made Spanish style solid body guitars with pickups, but none were commercially successful. However, Hawaiian style players quickly adopted the new technology.

Once a viable system was discovered, competition was swift. Gibson designed its own pickup, as did Epiphone and National. Others soon followed suit. They all realized that a significant change was taking place in how guitar music could be played and rushed to find systems that would compete with the Rickenbacker Electro without infringing on its patent. Their designs were based on magnetic wire coiled around a plastic bobbin with magnets underneath. A magnetic conducting material in the form of a bar or screws was inserted through the bobbin to transfer the magnetic field up from the magnets below to a position close to the guitar's strings.

While today's magnetic pickups may look different, be more powerful, and produce a wider variety of tones, they are all based on the same principles used by Beauchamp. The bar pickup, the Gibson P-90 with adjustable pole pieces, the Gibson Humbucker, the Gretsch Filtertron, and many

Hawaiian steel guitar with matching amplifier

more are just modifications and improvements; they are not new inventions.

Another key element was the creation of amplifiers. Sound amplification was originally developed for telephones, movies, phonographs, and radio. Beauchamp and Rickenbacker commissioned Roy Van Nest, who ran a radio shop in Los Angeles, to make a companion amplifier for the Electro solid body. Later they hired a design engineer to create more amplifiers. Eventually four models were available. All companies making electrified guitars sought to either make amplifiers or have them made by third parties.

This was all taking place in the depths of the Great Depression. With a peak of 25% unemployment and the collapse of banks and other institutions, many industries suffered, and guitar manufacturers were no exception. Gibson, for example, began shifting its excess capacity to the production of wooden toys.

Nevertheless, music of all sorts was still played, and the fascination with Hawaiian music continued unabated. Perhaps the exotic strains of Hawaii provided an escape from the fears of the Depression. Movies, after all, did quite well during this same time period. Escapism may be the tie that bound these two pastimes together. By the mid 1930s, Gibson, Epiphone, National, Kay, Harmony, and others were again making Hawaiian guitars, further popularizing the instruments.

As Europe began to descend into war, the Depression lifted in the United States. Soon, however, a scarcity of materials would limit the production of

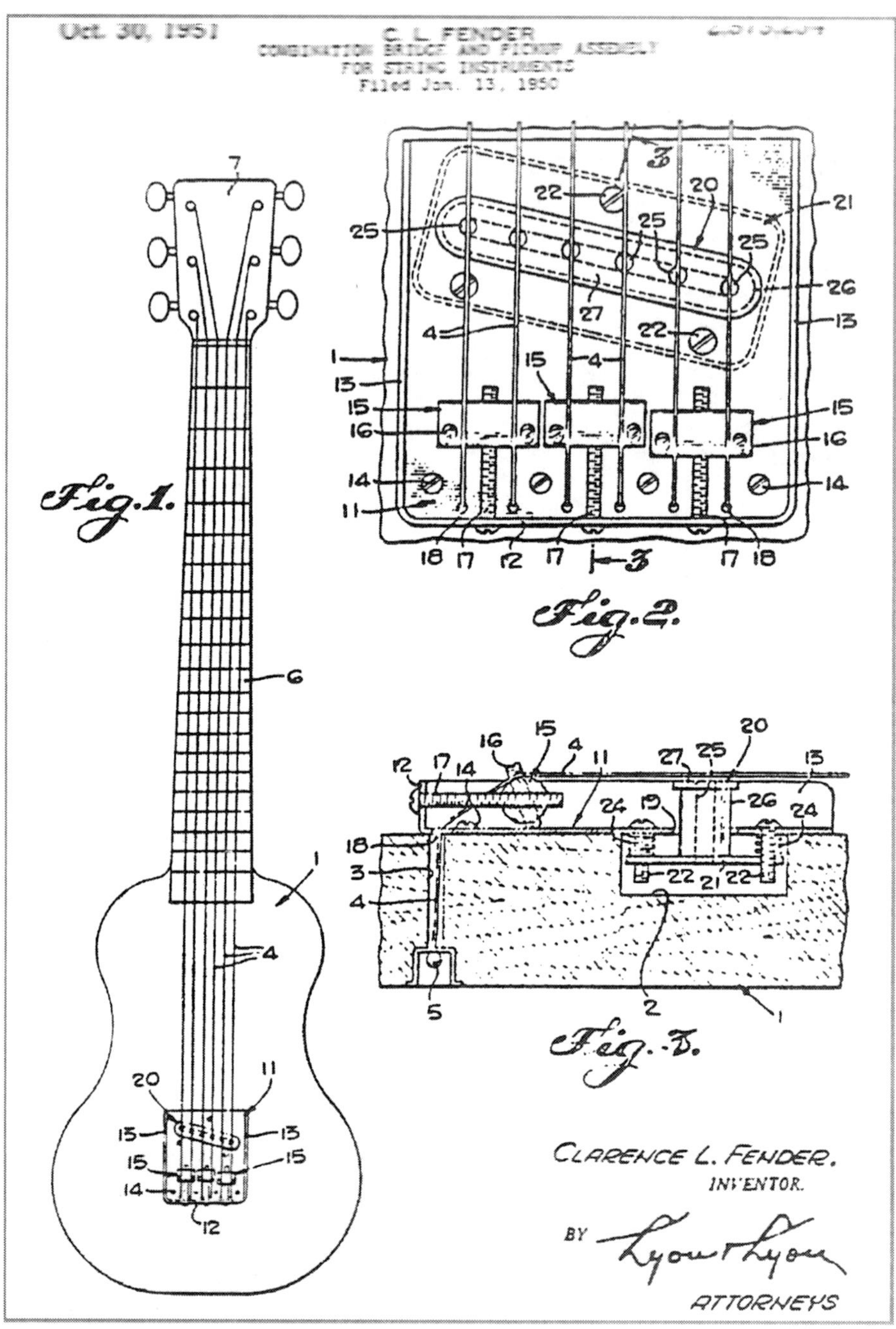

Leo Fender's Lap Steel design

all non-essentials. (I know many of you think of guitars as essential, but in the context of a global war, they were not.)

After very limited guitar production during World War II, guitar makers were quickly back in business. Manufacturers, Gibson, Epiphone, Kay, and others featured electric guitars in their post-war catalogues. Solid body Hawaiian instruments were prominently displayed.

Out in California, a fellow by the name of Leo Fender had set up a radio repair business during the war. In the back of his shop he built solid body Hawaiian guitars and the amplifiers necessary for them to make music. He and Doc Kaufman started K&F in 1945 to manufacture and market these products.

Fender would also build upon the work of George Beauchamp, but would do so using a design that both Gibson and Epiphone had previously tried and abandoned. This very simple system was to wrap the coil wire directly around the magnets themselves, each of which served as a pole piece sitting under one of the guitar's strings. Fender had perfected an inexpensive and easily manufactured pickup that worked beautifully. It is also fair to credit Fender with making a quantum leap in amplifier design. His amps combined power and tone in such a way that many believe they have never been improved upon.

There are several valid claims as to who made the "first" solid body electric setup for Spanish style guitar. Rickenbacker had made a Spanish style version of its Bakelite Style "B", Les Paul had built "the log", Audio-Vox had made both guitars and fretted solid body basses, and Paul Bigsby had made several solid bodies. But it was Leo Fender, the guy with the radio repair shop in California, who designed the first commercially successful example of the solid body electric Spanish style guitar—the Broadcaster—in 1950. That name was dropped after Gretsch protested its use (Gretsch had a line of drums and a banjo called the Broadkaster). After a brief period when the Fender creation had no model name (thus the designation as "the Nocaster"), it became the Telecaster in its two pickup form, and the Esquire when it was outfitted with just a bridge pickup.

The bolt-on neck solid body guitar was scoffed at when first introduced, but that derision soon turned to imitation. Leo Fender had taken the idea

1950 Broadcaster: the first commercially successful solid body "Spanish Style"

that had been first been successfully applied to the exotic music of the Pacific Islands and created the basic tool that would drive American popular music for many decades to come. The Gibson Les Paul followed in 1952; Fender created the three pickup sculpted-body Stratocaster in 1954, all soon to be followed by a remarkable burst of designs from Fender, Gibson, Gretsch, and others.

The age of rock and roll had begun, and its essential instrument, the electric guitar, was nearly perfected. Both hollow bodies and solid bodies were used in the early years of rock, but the true solid body became the essence of the rock sound. Here was a relatively inexpensive instrument that was loud enough to fill an auditorium with sound and shake the walls of many teenagers' bedrooms.

This was music accessible in ways that popular music had never been before. It was great to listen and dance to, and playing it was a real joy. Sure, it is hard to be Scotty Moore, who so brilliantly played with Elvis, but, as Dave Barry once said, "You can throw your guitar down the steps and it will play *Louie Louie*." The age of the garage band had been born.

Rock and roll is a uniquely American invention. Its amalgamation of European and African musical traditions could have happened nowhere else on earth, and its instrument of choice had roots from a small group of islands in the Pacific. Disparate people took a wide variety of influences, stirred them up, and out came a new form of music. Rock and roll would become one of America's greatest cultural exports.

When Jimi Hendrix got on that stage at Woodstock, when he blew the crowd away with skill, artistry, passion and volume, somewhere in the distance the dim strains of Hawaiian melodies and the whistle of a steamship could be heard.

CHAPTER THREE

But Who's Going to Play It?

There is a story from the early history of Nashville, Tennessee's Jewish community about someone who wanted to donate a chandelier to the Orthodox Jewish Congregation. This was a group founded by recent Eastern European immigrants with a somewhat limited knowledge of English and relatively limited experience of life in the United States. After hours of debate about the efficacy of accepting a chandelier, one member raised his hand and said, "Okay, maybe it's a good idea, but I got one question. Who's going to play it?"

While the story may be apocryphal and its only relationship to guitars may be that it took place in Music City, it does underscore an important aspect of the guitar industry. Guitars, like every other musical instrument, have very little value unless someone learns to play them. There are other products that require skill, but normally the skill level is low, or they are so ubiquitous, like automobiles, that learning to use them is seen as both normal and necessary.

Musical instruments, however, are seen by many as a nicety—an addition to life which may be worthwhile but certainly not essential. That is, of course, a generalization. For some, learning to play an instrument is as important as learning to read or do basic arithmetic. But that is not the norm in our society and has never been so. Nevertheless, musical instrument production and sales have been a constant in American culture and the various mechanisms and methods that people have used to teach people to play music have been both varied and fascinating. They range from the purely private to the very public.

A great deal of musical instrument production, sales, and instruction has been impacted by the range of options open for people to entertain themselves. We know that for human beings the urge to hear music is universal, but before the introduction of recorded (and later broadcast) music if people wanted instrumental music they had to either play it themselves or go somewhere where they could hear a live performance.

While there was formal music instruction available in churches and through professional teachers, a significant component of music instruction was and is informal—passed down from parent to child through generations. Through this process older styles of music have been kept alive and newer ones have been created. This instruction has encompassed singing, fiddle, guitar, piano, banjo, and every other sort of music making. It is difficult to chronicle because of the nature of its informality, yet impossible to ignore.

Formal music instruction in the United States was a private or church matter until the nineteenth century, a time when vocal and instrumental instruction was introduced into American public schools. The first music education in public schools, vocal instruction, was formalized in 1838 in Boston. Over the next hundred and fifty years band and orchestra programs would be added to the repertoire. In contrast, guitar instruction has only become a part of public school instruction since the late 1980s.

In the nineteenth century private guitar instruction was the norm. Most guitar sales in the early nineteenth century were to guitar teachers who would then turn around and sell the instruments to their students. A good deal of the distribution went through girls' schools. Prior to the Civil War, and for a significant time thereafter, the guitar was one of the instruments that was considered suitable for young ladies of a certain class, and guitar instruction became part of their school curriculum.

While there were music stores throughout the nineteenth century, teaching seemed to be the province of individual instructors or *professors*, as they were sometimes called. While the guitar may be the most popular musical instrument today, this was not true throughout the last two hundred years. Guitar playing was a niche in the musical landscape and not a terribly profitable one for large music stores. Thus instruction, and in many cases sales, was left to small independents.

Guitar playing was a proper activity for young girls

Several guitar instruction books were available in the 1800s. In 1855 the author of one of them wrote, "The object of this work is to offer the principles of the art of playing the guitar in the least possible space. Instead of dry exercises, which I think detrimental to the study of all beginners, I have, after the preliminary exercises, introduced pleasing airs of every description of style, with the various characters of expression, glides, harmonics and etc. as they occur in illustration." This author, as have many since, attempted to show that playing the guitar could be accomplished with ease and pleasure.

In another nineteenth century publication, *The Guitar: Without a Master*, the author writes of the balance between traditional musical education and teaching the guitar. "Unlike nearly all other instruments the guitar is mainly used in accompanying the voice and very few care to study it sufficiently to play difficult solos." So, more than a century ago the tension existed between the details of musicianship and its application to an instrument that is well suited to any level of difficulty.

This underscores a theme that will be repeated from the nineteenth century to the present day regarding guitars and guitar instruction. While the desire to make music may be nearly universal, the effort and tenacity required for someone to become an expert is not. The beauty of the guitar, which is matched by few other instruments, is that it can provide pleasure for both the player and audience at a variety of levels. The "guitar made easy" or "play guitar instantly" programs continued to be touted because they could address these different skill stages. Different styles of music and the goals of the students determined the level of instruction.

The latter part of the nineteenth century saw many additional changes in the musical landscape. The introduction of catalogues from Sears Roebuck & Co. and Montgomery Ward made instruments, including guitars, available to a broad swath of Americans. Many of these customers lived in rural areas where instruction was informal.

At this time there was also a rise in the performance of music by amateur groups and ensembles of every sort. This included classical music and marching music; every town seemed to have its own band. The new Gibson Mandolin Guitar Company capitalized on this trend with a new kind of marketing and instruction for fretted instruments.

Gibson was rather brilliant in its marketing efforts in the early 1900s. It sold its instruments to "teacher/agents" who would instruct students and sell them Gibson instruments. Gibson also introduced teaching materials to support instruction and encourage performance.

During the mandolin craze in America Gibson went far in its efforts to support it, expand it, and profit from it. Most significantly, this could be seen in the creation of mandolin orchestras. Here Gibson, taking a page from brass and woodwind instrument makers, created music for an entire range of mandolin style instruments. These included the mandolin, the mandocello, mandola, and mandobass. The latter three of these were instruments that Gibson specifically created to play in ensembles. They emulated the violin, viola, cello, and bass of the string quartet and, since the intervals were the same for all of the mandolin family instruments, the transition from one to the other was not difficult. Gibson had teaching materials and music specially written for mandolin orchestras, and featured their Gibson-created instruments in its advertising. The link between instrument sales and education became clear and direct.

This embrace and expansion of the fascination with mandolins underscores an important truth of the musical instrument universe. While Gibson did successfully expand the market for mandolin family instruments, it did not create it. The company responded to a demand from people who had been exposed to mandolin style music and wanted to play it. In virtually every case, the industry at all levels responds to consumer demand—it does not create it. Some sort of music engages the public—country, blues, rock and roll, folk, pop, or others—and the various arms of the instrument manufacturing and distribution chain work to fulfill, and perhaps expand, the resulting demand.

The end of the mandolin craze in the early 1920s was not, of course, the end of Gibson, but the company did struggle for a time. When they switched their marketing to focus on guitars and banjos, they once again enjoyed an increase in business. They continued to work with instructors to create and publish complete systems for guitar. The introduction to the company's 1939 instruction system is entitled "Happy Days for You." It reads, "The happiest days of your life are just ahead! …fun, friends, money, travel and your own personal pride are built all over once again you take up music." The promises made then, as now, may be hyperbolic, but for all who play music they underscored the truth.

The Gibson course was not a self-taught program. It was designed with the idea that the student would have a teacher who would explain and expand upon the written materials. Other programs, however, took a very

HAPPY DAYS FOR YOU

The happiest days of your life are just ahead!

A real thrill and joy that knows no bounds comes only through something you do yourself, and nothing in the whole world can compare with a self-made tune. This system brings "thrill a million" within your reach, just around the corner as it were, so step along lively and it won't be long until you actually feel the moment of a lifetime surge through your entire body.

Fun, friends, money, travel and your own personal pride are built all over again once you take up music.

You must live with yourself a long, long time, and to be able to pick up a musical instrument and soothe your injured feelings when sad or to play a smile back on your face, is something that only self-made music can do.

Music is not hard to learn, and this system will prove it.

Go after it right and musical success will be yours — nothing in the whole wide world can take it from you — it becomes you, a part of you night and day, year in and year out. Wherever you go, music is the one language that you can speak and be understood — it is everywhere.

Just a little serious effort on your part and with the help of this system, you will be started on the right road to playing tunes used by orchestras, soloists and combinations of all sorts.

Happy Days For You

different approach. In 1935 a *Five-Minute Guitar Book* was offered as a new and easy self-teaching method. With illustrations of chords, different ways to tune, and "25 chords and how to use them" this booklet was basic in its

instruction. While its promise of five-minute expertise may have been bold and unrealistic, it did give a basic introduction to first position chords and showed how to use them to play a variety of contemporary songs.

The popularity of Hawaiian music, which swept America in the early twentieth century, created its own instrument market and teaching industry. Hawaiian guitar music, much of which is played by sliding the bar to a variety of positions on an instrument tuned to an open tuning, was very easy to learn in its most simple form. It lent itself to self-instruction, and a variety of publishers stepped in to provide instructional materials. By the 1920s there were many Hawaiian music methods being published. The 1935 *Cole's Hawaiian Guitar Method* offered the "latest most modern up-to-date method for teaching the Hawaiian guitar." The ukulele was also extremely popular and sales of the instruments and accompanying instruction books were very strong.

The largest of all the Hawaiian instruction systems came from the Oahu Publishing Company of Cleveland, Ohio. Oahu had courses for both self-teaching and instructor use. They also offered a full line of instruments and accessories and reams of sheet music designed specifically for the Hawaiian guitar. Their in-house magazine *The Guitarist* was, they claimed, the only magazine published that was devoted exclusively to the guitar. It was cleverly, and somewhat blatantly, slanted toward the marketing of Oahu and Oahu products. The company built its reputation on the Hawaiian guitar and was slow to make the transition to the more traditional Spanish-style, so it soon slid into oblivion.

At its height, however, Oahu was a major force in musical instruction and instrument sales. There are thousands of instruments existing today with the Oahu label, but none of these were actually made by the company.

Their guitars and amplifiers came from a variety of manufacturers who would apply the Oahu brand to them. They ranged from the most basic to the beautiful and ornate. In 1939, the "Oahu Deluxe Jumbo Guitar: the Aristocrat of Them All" came in both a square neck and round neck version at a cost of $158. Credit terms were available and the company would also accept trade-ins. For comparison sake, in 1939 a Martin D-28 sold for $100 without a case. The ability of Oahu to package instruments and accessories with both their comprehensive teaching packages and music gave them a somewhat captive market in an era when there were not the abundant alternatives available today.

Oahu's instructional materials were complete and covered everything from the most basic beginners' tuning and strumming to very complex arrangements made for the expert. Oahu promised that with your new skill and expertise, which would be acquired with ease and joy, you would become the life of the party and popularity would be assured. More important, however, Oahu made the same argument put forth by Gibson, public schools, and private instructors—music would enhance one's life.

The 1950s and '60s saw fundamental change in guitar instruction because it saw fundamental change in music itself. The guitar became the country's most popular instrument, supplanting piano, home organ, and the accordion.

The guitar had earlier been used for jazz, blues, country, and other forms of music, but in the 1950s new musical genres emerged that made an ever-increasing number of young people want to play it. The first wave of explosive growth was rock and roll. This brilliant blend of blues, country, and gospel was dominated by guitars and lent itself to emulation. Certainly it is not easy to become a Scotty Moore, who played on many of Elvis's great recordings, but it is relatively simple to play three or four chords and form your very own rock band. Here was a perfect form of music that combined the rebellion of youth with relative ease of playing.

The second genre that took hold in America was the folk boom of the late 1950s. Here too true expertise might be difficult to attain, but many young people found that three or four chords were enough to allow them to participate in the folk revival. The Beatles era in the early 1960s led to an exponential growth in the popularity of guitar music and guitar playing that

Instant popularity from Oahu

would be difficult to overstate. The guitar became a major part of American instrument production and sales.

The quarter-century after the Second World War was a tumultuous time in American politics, culture, economics, and social trends. The era was

The great jazz player Tal Farlow

composed of an odd mixture of confidence and fear. The United States had emerged from the war as one of the two big "superpowers" that now dominated much of world economics, and was now the leader of what came to be called the "free world." There was also a palpable sense of fear in an age where "mutually assured destruction" was a new normalcy.

Added to this was a younger generation who tended to reject many of the social norms and traditions of their parents. The very size of this group gave them a kind of legitimacy, or at least a perceived power, that was a new twist on generational antipathy. Change seemed to be coming rapidly and unpredictably. The assassinations of John F. Kennedy and Martin Luther King Jr., the Vietnam War, "Flower Power," the sexual revolution, and other issues heightened the sense of disquiet.

PART ONE

MELODY LANE

MURRAY SISTERS
Radio-Records

Start Right Play A Tune

THERE is a world of fun ahead for you and your friends with music. Start now to travel this "Road to Happiness" — be like thousands of others who are already playing guitar and enjoying the friendship of music.

You will be surprised at the speed with which you learn to play. Very soon now, you will be playing for your friends, so urge them to start lessons and you can all play together.

GEORGE SMITH
Paramount Studios, Hollywood

YOU CAN PLAY THIS SPANISH GUITAR SOLO *TODAY!*

HOOSIER HOT SHOTS
N B C Chicago

GLEN GRAY and
JACK BLANCHETTE
Casa Loma Orchestra

GENE AUTRY
Movies, Radio, Records

GIBSON SYSTEM FOR GUITAR

Basic instruction

Mel Bay

Rock and roll lent itself to this rebellion and, in some ways, exacerbated it. Once again the issue of race had emerged from the shadows of American history, and by the mid-1950s it was a dominant issue in American society and politics. Rock and roll was associated with African-American music, and for that reason was embraced by some and rejected by others. The music also elicited a sensuality that was more open than that of previous eras. Virtually all of the front men in rock and roll played guitars and the instrument virtually defined the folk era.

Along with guitar-based music came the standalone guitar store. Ernie Ball claims to have had the first dedicated guitar store in California in the late 1950s. Prior to this, guitars were sold in full-line music stores that sold all manner of instruments. Over the next decade, guitar stores would proliferate, and as they did, many of them incorporated instruction into their repertoire. It was clear to them, and the music industry in general, that the health of guitar sales depended upon expanding the base of players, and that was largely a function of guitar instruction.

There was also an expansion of what we would today call "distance learning," and an increase in self-guided instruction books and methods. Mel Bay, Hal Leonard, and many smaller companies have offered books for both beginners and more advanced students for many years. Changes in technology have produced corresponding changes in the types of media available for teaching. These books would sometimes come with records, which later became cassettes, which later became CDs, which later became DVDs, which have now become available online.

Happy Traum began Homespun Tapes in 1967. The company first offered instruction on cassettes, and later came to embrace VHS tape and DVD.

Before cassettes, CDs, VHSs, DVDs, and downloads there were these floppy records

Interestingly, Traum says, before introducing video instruction he had surveyed his cassette customers, and they overwhelmingly rejected video. Nevertheless, Traum began to release VHS lessons and found them to be very successful. While the company has grown to offer a wide variety of programs on many instruments, some of which are quite advanced, a significant portion of their sales are to near-beginners. These are people who may know how to hold the guitar, how to tune it, and play a few chords, but want the ease and convenience of video lessons at home. Companies like Homespun, therefore, play a significant role in nurturing the new player.

The computer age has produced a new wave of lessons that are available at a variety of prices, starting at, well, free. These can be streamed instantly to a

Homespun has been in the "distance learning" business for many years.

prospective student. Some are by rather well-known instructors, while others are by lesser-known but talented teachers who see an opening with this new technology. Others are simply put out there by people who believe they have something to offer. We live in an age of overwhelming information, and the difficulty that we face is in sorting it all out. With so many instructional options it is not easy to find one that best suits an individual student. Music store instruction, private instructors, and well-established lesson companies still have a dynamic place to play in the creation of good guitar players. Like an instrument that is so poorly made that it cannot be played well, instruction that is poorly designed and/or delivered does not offer someone the best chance to become a successful guitar player at any level.

One great anomaly here is that neither the Guitar Center nor the Sam Ash chains of stores have offered lessons until recently. Today both have adopted many of the tools of the smaller independent guitar shops which offer lessons and opportunities for students to perform. The lesson programs from guitar stores provide two important elements. First they are an income stream in themselves, and secondly the students are often the best customers for instruments and accessories as they progress.

The management of both chains have come to realize the importance of lessons. Throughout much of the late twentieth century some guitar stores were able to rely on others to provide the teaching. They would offer a large selection of instruments at low prices. There was a belief that people would learn guitar playing on their own, through private instruction, or from that offered by independent guitar shops. Once they were introduced to the instrument they would then come to the "big box store" to upgrade their instruments. As music has changed significantly in the late twentieth and into the twenty-first century, that assumption is no longer viable. Young people today have a vast array of options from which to choose for their leisure and aesthetic fulfillment. Playing the guitar, or any other traditional instrument, is not a default position. It must be encouraged and nurtured.

Guitar instruction in the United States since the nineteenth century to the present day has reflected both great change and consistency. The method of delivery has changed dramatically. Yet, even as digital downloads and streaming have increased in popularity, the need and desire for some people to have personal instruction continues. It is now rare that a guitar shop, or any music store for that matter, will not have an active lesson program. From the guitar "professors" of the nineteenth century to the 6' x 8' teaching studio of today, personal instruction continues to have a useful place.

Like most things, the popularity of guitars and guitar music is always in a state of flux. It changes as new musical forms rise and fall, as entertainment internet guitar instruction

Web Videos Shopping Maps Images More ▾ Search tools

About 956,000 results (0.31 seconds)

Ad related to **internet guitar instruction**

Top 10 **Guitar** Programs - We Exposed the Top **Guitar Lessons**
www.**onlinelesson**reviews.com/**Guitar** ▾
Which Ones Made the Cut? Read More!

Justin Guitar | Free **Guitar Lessons**
justin**guitar**.com/ ▾ Justin Sandercoe
Completely free **guitar lessons** from Justin Sandercoe including beginners, electric, acoustic, blues, rock, jazz, folk, technique, aural training and a whole lot ...
Beginner's Course - Song Lessons - Lesson Index - Intermediate Method

Guitar Lessons (100% FREE) - Learn How To Play Guitar Online
www.**guitarlessons**.com/ ▾
This website features both acoustic **guitar lessons** and electric **guitar lessons** that ... It is the largest source of free video **guitar lessons** available on the **internet**.
Guitar Lessons - Beginner Guitar Quick-Start ... - Guitar Chords - Jam Tracks

Beginner **Guitar Lessons** - About.com
guitar.about.com/library/bl**guitarlesson**archive.htm ▾
Learning to play guitar is a challenge, but with this series of **free online guitar lessons**, complete with popular songs to practice, you'll begin to improve ...

Internet Guitar Lessons | Learn Guitar with Tim Miller
members.**internetguitarlessons**.tv/ ▾
Internet Guitar Lessons · Home · Member Login · Join Today! Lessons · Forum · Extras · Terms ... Learn how to play music with guitarist Tim Miller. Tim Video Pic ...
Lesson Directory - Member Login - Terms Of Use - Join Today!

How To Learn Guitar - 8 Important **Guitar Lessons** For Beginners ... 
www.youtube.com/watch?v... ▾ YouTube
May 3, 2011 - Uploaded by flyers821
http://jamguitar.**net** - Hey looking for a great way to learn guitar? These 8 important **guitar lessons** for ...
9:52

Vanderbilly | **Free Online** Video **Guitar Lessons**
www.vanderbilly.com/ ▾
LICKS, RIFFS, SONGS, SOLOS. **LEARN** TO PLAY **GUITAR**. We have the largest and fastest growing collection of free **instructional guitar** videos in the world.

Online **Guitar Lessons**
www.**guitar**tricks.com/ ▾
Learn to play guitar with electric **guitar lessons**, acoustic **guitar lessons**, over 300 ... I don't think there is a better deal on the **Internet** than GuitarTricks.com.

Riff Interactive - Online **Guitar Lessons**
www.riffinteractive.com/ ▾
live online **guitar lessons**, advanced music notation software, **guitar lesson** ... I have looked all around the **Internet** for something that looks and feels right.

What are some good **free online guitar lessons**? - Yahoo Answers
answers.yahoo.com › ... › Entertainment & Music › Music › Other - Music ▾
Jan 7, 2011 - Hello there, There are a lot of good **instructional** materials available on-line. Here is some that I like. Video **lessons**. This guy has a series of 12 ...

Free Online Guitar Lessons - How To Tune A Guitar
www.howtotune**aguitar**.org/**lessons**/ ▾
Free Online Guitar Lessons. Learning to play the guitar to a very high level can take years. But if you are a beginner guitar player, you can learn to play guitar on ...

Searches related to **internet guitar instruction**

free internet guitar **lessons** **free online bass** guitar **lesson**

Ads

Free **Online Guitar Lesson**
www.**guitar**tricks.com/Free-**Lessons** ▾
Play Your First Solo in 15 Minutes!
This Simple Trick Makes **Guitar** Easy

Online Guitar Courses
www.**web**crawler.com/ ▾
Search multiple engines for
online guitar courses

MTSU **Online**
www.mtsu**online**.com/ ▾
1 (615) 494 7714
Take Classes **Online** or On Campus
Flexible Custom Designed Degrees

Online Guitar Instruction
www.ask.com/**Online+Guitar+Instruction** ▾
Find **Online Guitar Instruction**;
Online at Ask.com. Try It Now!

Franklin School of Rock
www.franklin.schoolofrock.com/ ▾
1 (615) 221 9700
Guitar, Bass, Keys, Drums, Vocals
Performance Based **Instruction**

Rock Class 101
www.rockclass101.com/ ▾
Online Guitar Bass and Drum **Lessons**
14 Day Free Trial!

Online Music **Lessons**
www.songbird-music.com/ ▾
Search for teachers from around the world for live, **online lessons**.

Learn **Guitar Online**
www.nyc**guitar**school.com/learn-**online** ▾
Revolutionary 10 Week Course
Signup Today!

See your ad here »

Google Search "Guitar Instruction"

and creative options increase, and as technology changes. One thing that remains constant, however, is that if a guitar or any musical instrument is to have utility someone has to learn to play it.

Shortcuts have been conceived and tried, but to date these have been mere flashes in the pan. "Guitar Hero," a game with a guitar-shaped controller, was one of these, and was very popular when first introduced. It caused quite a stir in the guitar industry. Would this guitar simulator replace or at least diminish actual guitar playing or, on the other hand, would it become a gateway for people to learn how to actually play the instrument? It turned out that neither of these scenarios played out. "Guitar Hero" came and went. It is difficult to know all of the reasons for its sudden demise, but it is fair to speculate that the experience did not satisfy the need for people to be creative. It was merely a game that tested the ability of the player to mimic music—not make it.

Some other technology may come about that will be both easy to master and fulfilling to the creative impulse that leads people to play actual instruments, but we have yet to see it. Until we do, there will be a need for instructors and instructional methods to pass along skill, passion, and expertise.

CHAPTER FOUR

The Odd Couple

Two small niche music markets combined to expand the popularity and use of guitars in American music during the 1920s and '30s. In some ways these two forms of music—hillbilly (later called country), which was aimed toward a rural white audience, and blues, which was directed towards a rural African-American audience—would seem to be worlds apart. This was, after all, a time when the racial divide in the United States was seemingly a brick wall. Certainly this was true in regard to politics and many social interactions, but when it came to music and the economics of music, the wall was permeable.

The introduction of records and later, radio, changed the way people could listen to music. For the first time ever, people could hear music that they did not either play themselves or go somewhere to hear it live. This was a revolution that caused permanent change in the economics of music and the spread of musical tastes. In the United States hillbilly and blues were both beneficiaries of these new media.

Lower production costs and wider distribution methods allowed record companies to make money catering to these relatively small markets. It was not dissimilar from the "narrow casting" we see today with cable and now Internet video. Lower costs allowed small markets, like blues and hillbilly, to turn a profit, much as a cable channel devoted to either cooking, playing golf or decorating a home can succeed today. In the 1920s a general pop or swing record could sell millions of copies but hillbilly and blues records selling 10,000 were considered to be hits. Some artists, such as blues singers Ma Rainey and Bessie Smith, and hillbilly singer Vernon Dalhart, sold many more than that, but they were the wild exceptions to the rule.

Record companies like Okeh began to produce "race records" in the early 1920s which were aimed at the rural African-American audience. Early blues recordings featured the powerful vocals of Rainey and Smith backed by full bands. A 1923 Okeh Records release of blues singer Sarah Martin accompanied by Sylvester Weaver on guitar was advertised as "the first blue guitar record." It would not be the last. Starting in 1926 Blind Lemon Jefferson gained wide acceptance when his "Long Lonesome Blues" sold over 100,000 copies. Blind Willie McTell, the Memphis Jug Band, and other performers made numerous records and traveled along a juke joint circuit that spread their music. The light that shines above all others in this genre is Robert Johnson, who recorded in the late 1930s, after the heyday of guitar-based country blues. This legendary guitar player, singer, and composer left a mark that has only increased in intensity over time, although he never enjoyed the commercial success of Jefferson. The guitar styles of Jefferson, Johnson, and legions of others began to carve out a new role for the instrument.

The profitability of "race records" led to the almost accidental discovery of another niche market—rural white people. In 1923 Okeh recorded and released "Little Old Log Cabin," a fiddle tune from John Carson. This became an unexpected money maker and confirmed the economic viability of hillbilly music. The label recorded the tune incidentally while it was in Atlanta to tape some "race records," and recorded Carson as an afterthought.

Other hillbilly recordings soon followed, as record companies continued to send people to the South to discover and record new artists. Nineteen twenty-seven was a seminal year in hillbilly/country music history. It was then that Ralph Peer set up his equipment in Bristol, Tennessee and recorded some of the most important names in the genre. Both Jimmie Rodgers and the Carter Family were part of the Bristol sessions—after this, hillbilly/country music would never be the same.

Early hillbilly music had been primarily dance music played on fiddle and banjo, similar to the style of John Carson. Guitars were used, but they were not the featured instruments. This changed with Rogers and the Carter Family, and the many musicians who would follow in their footsteps. Guitars would finally begin to take center stage.

Blind Lemon Jefferson

John Carson and his daughter

Jimmie Rodgers was the first major solo star in country music. His unique "blue yodel" encouraged a wave of imitators and inventors who would take hillbilly singing and guitar playing in new directions. Riley Puckett, Vernon Dalhart, Carson Robison, the Stonemans, and other hillbilly singers either accompanied themselves or were accompanied by guitars.

The Carter Family, featuring Maybelle Carter on guitar, broke even more new ground. With her unique style, she introduced the guitar as a lead instrument in hillbilly/country music, and showed that it could provide both rhythm and lead lines. It would be hard to find an American acoustic guitar player who has not tried to play her rendition of "Wildwood Flower." She was key in raising the guitar to its central position in this style of music and, by extension, many others.

The guitar had always been used to accompany the human voice, a task for which it is well suited. This association grew with the popularity of hillbilly and blues. The guitar's ability to reflect and support vocals was an important element in its growing recognition. Maybelle had shown that the guitar could provide the driving rhythm of a banjo and the melody of the fiddle. Rogers and others proved that a solo singer playing a guitar could bring power and emotion to a song. And when combined with a slide, the guitar perfectly enhanced the moaning of the blues.

The Carter Family—Mother Maybelle with her Gibson L-5

The guitar was not the only instrument to rise in popularity in the 1920s. The mandolin transitioned from its earlier applications to country music. In particular, duos featuring mandolin and guitar became fashionable. The steel guitar also shifted from its Hawaiian music roots to country and blues.

The musical link between white hillbilly music and African-American blues music is well documented. The connection between Jimmie Rodgers's music, for example, and that of the African-American community is clear and direct. His music was a synthesis of musical styles that transcended race.

There was also an economic union that is less well known, and, given the racial tenor of the times, somewhat odd. RCA's Bluebird label, the Okeh label, and the Vocalion label, all purveyors of low-cost recordings, sold hillbilly and "race records" together in one brochure. This was in no way meant to be a statement about racial harmony, but rather a statement about music

Bluebird was RCA's budget brand for niche music

and money. White and black America may have had massive barriers to social interaction, but it was certainly permissible for companies to intermix their marketing literature aimed at small markets.

Radio was the second innovation that spread guitar music. Once songs hit the airwaves there was a corresponding decline in record sales, particularly among the poor in rural America. Record players were often as expensive as a radio, and the records themselves were fragile, so rural people found that radio was a far better investment for their entertainment. The purchase of one radio set could bring them music that would remain current without additional expense. The decline in record sales was particularly acute after the Depression started, when numbers plummeted from over 104 million in 1927 to 6 million in 1932.

Hillbilly music spread throughout the United States via radio in ways that blues did not. Radio stations did host some African-American artists (Duke Ellington had his own show by the late 1920s), but the variety "barn dance" format that did so much to promote country music did not exist with blues or jazz. Although hillbilly music had a difficult time breaking into radio, it was, after all, white. Blues and jazz, of course, came out of African-American culture and had a much harder time reaching American airwaves. Many radio station owners believed that the new medium should be used for educational and other popularly-accepted purposes, so religious, classical, opera, and similar forms were dominant.

RADIO RECEIVERS

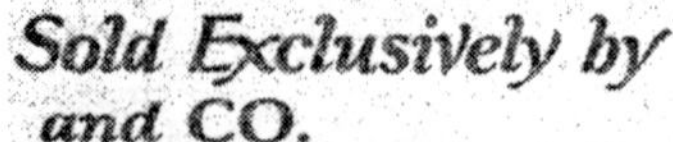

The radio assembly embraces the Tuned Radio Frequency Circuit. It is strong, rugged and reflects symmetry and precision in engineering. Contains no parts likely to get out of order. All sockets for the five tubes are mounted on a heavy, floating type subbase. Solid steel panel to match cabinets. Three neatly decorated tuning dials, volume control and switch. Easy to set up and operate. No radio knowledge necessary. We guarantee complete satisfaction.

$6.00 Down
$6.00 Monthly

$34.95
CASH
WITHOUT ACCESSORIES

Model XV

You may prefer this receiver, as the use of a separate loud speaker is not required. The built-in sound chamber is of ample size and is designed along lines that make for remarkable results. It is fitted with a heavy metal throat to which is attached a large modern type reproducing unit that will stand heavy volume with wonderful tone quality. We guarantee you complete satisfaction. The cabinet is made of selected gumwood, dark mahogany finish. It measures 30½ inches long, 10¾ inches deep and 9 inches high. Equipped with our regular Silvertone five-tube radio assembly.

Model XV Silvertone Receiver only, without accessories. Shipping weight, 40 pounds.

57K2792¼—Cash price $34.95

57K2793¼—Easy payment price, **$6.00** cash with order and **$6.00** per month until paid $36.50

Model XV Silvertone Receiver, complete with all accessories (ready to set up and operate), including five detector-amplifier storage battery tubes, two large heavy duty 45-volt "B" batteries, one voltmeter (for testing "B" batteries), one 100-ampere-hour storage battery, one battery tester (for testing storage battery), complete aerial and ground equipment. Shipping weight, 145 pounds.

57K2794¼—Cash price $59.95

57K2795¼—Easy payment price, **$9.00** cash with order and **$9.00** per month until paid $65.95

When ordering on Time Payments use Time Payment Order Blank on page 1092.

$59.95
CASH, Without Accessories

$9.00 Down
$9.00 Monthly

Model XVII

Console type cabinet with a complete built-in sound chamber set above the radio assembly. Made of genuine mahogany, which has a rich, hand rubbed finish. Two-tone trim. Removable panel in front of battery compartment. Radio assembly mounted on a pull-out slide, affording ready access to the tubes. Height of console, 44½ inches; width, across the front, 25 inches; depth, 13¼ inches.

Model XVII Silvertone Radio Console only, without accessories. Shipping weight, 100 pounds.

57K2800¼—Cash price $59.95

57K2801¼—Easy payment price, **$9.00** cash with order and **$9.00** per month until paid $65.95

Model XVII Silvertone Receiver, complete with all accessories (ready to set up and operate), including five detector-amplifier storage battery tubes, two large heavy duty 45-volt "B" batteries, one voltmeter (for testing "B" batteries), one 100-ampere-hour storage battery, one battery tester (for testing storage battery), complete aerial and ground equipment. Shipping weight, 205 pounds.

57K2802¼—Cash price $84.95

57K2803¼—Easy payment price, **$13.00** cash with order and **$13.00** per month until paid $92.95

When ordering on Time Payments use Time Payment Order Blank on page 1092.

See Index and Information Pages 542 to 570 709

1927 Sears Radio offerings

In many ways the radio itself was indiscriminate. The signal was sent out to anyone who could receive it. Yet, there was an intimacy associated with it since the physical radio set was in the privacy of one's home. True, recordings were also played at home, but it was a conscious act to bring those recordings home and play them. In the early days of radio, where there was not nearly the choice available later, there was a great sense that radio content had to be strictly governed. Hillbilly may have been seen as low class, but blues and jazz were viewed as foreign and profane so were even less welcome on American airwaves.

Radio stations in Chicago, Atlanta, Wheeling, Nashville, and mega-stations along the Mexican border spread the music of hillbilly performers from the Mexican border to the upper Midwest. Nashville's Grand Ole Opry was not the first barn dance program, but it has certainly become the most famous. The Opry was introduced as a short barn dance program by George Hay, who had earlier been a radio announcer in Chicago. Nashville radio station WSM, whose owners reluctantly allowed the first broadcast, was overwhelmed by the response and continued to expand the offerings on its barn dance program. Advertisers in Nashville and in many other markets found that the integration of their products with hillbilly music and humor was an effective way to increase their sales. These barn dance programs brought artists like Jimmie Rodgers and the Carter Family into many homes throughout the United States.

Changes in music and the American economy led to an increase in guitar production at all levels. Martin, for whom we have the best corporate records, went from producing 910 guitars in 1921 to 5,566 guitars in 1927. Gibson too increased its production of six-stringed instruments. This company, which had focused on mandolins and similar instruments earlier in its existence, had a difficult transition to make after the mandolin craze faded. In response to this, the company expanded its guitar offerings in the late 1920s and 1930s. Both Martin and Gibson designed new instruments or modified existing ones to meet changing musical tastes.

Lloyd Loar, Gibson's legendary instrument designer, introduced the first F-hole archtop at Gibson in 1923, less for its own sake than to complete his quartet of archtop mandolin style instruments. This guitar, the L5, was used by several hillbilly and later Western players, but its main application was in big band, jazz, and swing, music that was sweeping urban America at the time.

c. 1927 Gibson L-1

Both Martin and Gibson made changes to flat top guitars—nearly all of them used the steel strings that had become popular during the boom in Hawaiian music. Guitar music continued to evolve from classical finger style to jazz, country, and other sorts of music. In these genres where steel-string instruments were more appropriate, players more often used flat picks and closed chords. Martin gradually switched to steel strings in the early 1920s, introduced the 14-fret guitar in 1929, and began to make the large dreadnought guitar under their own name in 1931. Gibson, for its part, introduced a wide range of flat top steel-string guitars, including the L-1, the L-00 in the 1920s, and its own large Jumbo series in 1934. All of these innovations were made to meet the demands of new music and new customers. Other companies including Gretsch and Harmony were soon to follow suit.

The resonator guitar, which uses a metal cone to make its signature sound, was invented by the Dopyera brothers in 1927. It was a successful attempt to make a guitar louder than the traditional flat top and archtop designs allowed. While today it is most often associated with blues and country music, it was used for many forms of music throughout the 1930s, a period when different sorts of instruments were used in all styles of guitar music.

While hillbilly and blues singers helped create a growing demand for guitars in general and steel-string flattops in particular, they were not the only people who played these instruments. Pop singers such as Nick Lucas, who lent his name to one Gibson model, also propelled guitars to the front of the stage. Roy Smeck, "The Wizard of Strings," also popularized guitars, along with ukes, banjos, and steels. Guitar players like Eddie Lang also broke new ground in jazz, and was one of many outstanding musicians accompanying very popular singers.

Records and radio playing both hillbilly and blues elevated guitars in American music. This was accompanied by a rise in the American consumer economy brought about by the introduction of new products based on the ever-widening availability of electricity. The economy was also aided by more efficient industrial techniques that provided cheaper products, an expansion of wealth (which came to an abrupt end with the Great Depression), and a distribution system that allowed both rural and urban Americans easier access to products. In urban areas stores were flush with new consumer products, while rural America depended on the U.S. Mail and burgeoning catalog sales for access to this burgeoning market.

The Sears Roebuck and Montgomery Ward catalogs played a huge role in rural American buying habits. A look through old issues of these "department stores in print" shows the wealth of goods that were available. Guitars grew in the absolute number of instruments offered and their relative position in the context of all instruments. In 1927 the Sears catalog offered 9 guitars, 15 violins, and 21 accordions. By 1930 guitar offerings had increased to 13, violins were down to 10, and there were only 15 accordions. By 1938 the catalog listed 16 guitars, including arch tops, 14 accordions, and but 8 violins. This trend seems to reflect the relative popularity of these instruments over time beyond the realm of catalog sales.

Roy Smeck "The Wizard of Strings"

One of the great anomalies in American cultural history is the growth of rural-based music at the same time when America was statistically becoming more urban. In 1900 more than 60% of Americans were rural, by 1920 this figure dropped to 48%, and by 1940 it had declined to 43.5%. Many musical trends, including jazz and big band music, catered to a sophisticated urban clientele. Hillbilly and blues, however, found their audiences among people who either lived in rural America or had recently come from it. Newcomers to the city brought their rural roots with them.

Sears guitar offerings

The themes of hillbilly music were often those of loss and deprivation. This loss was not only personal loss of love, but also a seeming loss of a way of life. While for many it had been a life of subsistence or grinding poverty, it was the life they had known and still cherished—if only in memory. Music underscored the value of a rural life that was rapidly fading in importance.

Okeh Race and Hillbilly catalogue

Once they migrated to the cities, country people often found that factory work was their only option. Here too the work was grinding and many of them were barely able to survive. There was a comfort in music that reminded them of their roots—of a time when the independent farmer was central to American life. The United States had begun as an agricultural country with a feeling of distrust of cities and manufacture among some of its inhabitants. Thomas Jefferson had called farmers "God's chosen people on earth" and had famously said "Let Europe be our workshop." But with industrialization rural life was becoming yesterday's news.

Music doesn't deal in reality. Instead, it evokes feelings and passions that span beyond the intellectual. Hillbilly music played this role for many of Americans in the 1920s and 1930s. In a sense it validated their longing for a life left behind. It was comfortable, it was entertaining, and it was familiar.

The blues, while having rural roots, did not reflect on "the good old days" with nostalgic longing. Instead, the music often spoke of the ordeals of poverty and the effects of rampant racism that confronted people whose parents remembered slavery and were submerged in a society that viewed African-Americans with contempt.

Both hillbilly music and blues would evolve as their respective audiences were impacted by their new urban environments. Yet, many of the themes would remain constant. Hillbilly, and later country music, would continue to express ideas based on farming, individualism, and faith. Blues would continue to stress loss, deprivation, discrimination, and sexuality.

Hillbilly became country and the raw blues of Blind Lemon Jefferson and Robert Johnson formed the basis of jazz, swing, the electric blues of Chicago and the West Coast, and rock and roll. Both of these transformations would lead to the creation of a musical instrument industry that would, particularly after the mid-1960s, become increasingly based on fretted instruments.

Hillbilly and blues are inexorably intertwined musically. They are intertwined economically and socially as well. While the barrier was thick between the two races in the American South, where both of these forms of music grew and blossomed, it was a barrier filled with holes.

Both forms of this rural-based music reflected a society with limited industry and technology, yet both depended on the new technologies of the twentieth century to spread. Much of the rural South had to wait for the New Deal of the 1930s to obtain electricity. There are two ironies here: the most segregated part of the United States, the South, was home to a racial interchange central to American culture, and the musical forms that emerged from this primarily rural agricultural region were tied to the cutting edge technologies of urban America.

As the nation entered the decade of the 1940s and '50s the issue of race would come welling up throughout American society. The country would come face-to-face with the unresolved issues that were the legacy of slavery and the Civil War. Music had been one area where the two cultures came together almost from their first meeting, and it would soon play a significant role in the era of civil rights. Rock and roll in particular encouraged whites and blacks to share the same places while listening to the same music. It was a phenomenon that would bring a younger generation together at the same time that it often terrified their elders. The very obvious and open amalgamation of white and black music of the 1950s and '60s did not emerge full-blown in its own time. Instead, it was an extension of the musical and economic relationships that had been part of white and black music for generations.

CHAPTER FIVE

Westward Ho!

In the 1960s Mason Williams was a writer and guitar player for the satirical "Smothers Brothers Comedy Hour" who had recently had an instrumental hit with his piece "Classical Gas." At the time the Federal Communications Commission was investigating television and its role in the youth rebellion against the Vietnam War and a variety of other issues, and Williams was called to testify. He pulled out his guitar and sang a song he had written entitled "Cowboy Buckaroo." His premise was that his generation had grown up watching cowboys on TV who would stand up to do what was right no matter what the odds. This was a common theme in Westerns—one person standing up to many with the certitude of rightness on his side. While it may have been disconcerting to the house members, there was an essential truth to Williams's testimony.

One of the basic elements of the romanticized cowboy image is his inherent individualism. This is, to a large degree, a reflection of the Protestant ethic that infuses American culture. Protestantism is the most individualistic of any Western religion. Catholicism, Judaism, and Islam are all fundamentally based on group activities. Protestantism, on the other hand, gives the individual a direct relationship to the divine, and places responsibility for his or her own salvation on that connection. To Protestants this is an individual act of faith, and it is a fundamental belief that informs American culture, politics, and economics. It can easily be argued that both capitalism and a belief in democracy itself are largely an outgrowth of Protestant theology. The idealized lone cowboy is another manifestation of this.

The Western image is a compelling one in American social history. From the late nineteenth century onward there has been a romance imparted to the

Cowboy Buckaroos

1. I was raised on matinees ev'ry Saturday afternoon,
Lookin' up at Hoppy, Gene and Roy (Oh boy!)
And I grew up a-thinkin' the best a man can do
Is be a rootin' tootin' straight shootin' Cowboy Buckaroo.

    Spurs a-jangle-in', whoopy ti-yi-yay,
    Just a-wrangle-in' through ev'ry single day —
    Idle leedle lady, odle leedle lady,
    Idle leedle lady odle hoo —
    A man should be a rootin' tootin' straight shootin' Cowboy Buckaroo.

2. A Buckaroo's a cowboy who believes in what is good.
A Buckaroo wouldn't hurt you if he could (if he could).
I ain't afraid to say it, 'cause I ain't afraid of you —
I'm a rootin' tootin' straight shootin' Cowboy Buckaroo.

    Spurs a-jangle-in', whoopy ti-yi-yay,
    Just a-wrangle-in' through ev'ry single day(-a-lodle-lady) —
    Idle leedle lady, odle leedle lady,
    Idle leedle lady odle hoo —
    I'm a rootin' tootin' straight shootin' Cowboy Buckaroo.

3. Should we be the way we are, or be how we could be?
Could the movies become reality?
I'd like to ask a question, the answer's overdue:
Why don't we all ride together and be Cowboy Buckaroos?

    Spurs a-jangle-in', whoopy ti-yi-yay,
    Just a-wrangle-in' through ev'ry single be-yodel-ful day —
    Idle leedle lady, odle leedle lady,
    Idle leedle lady odle hoo —
    Why don't we all ride together and be Cowboy Buckaroos?

(ENDING)

    Idle leedle lady, odle leedle lady,
    Idle leedle lady odle lady hoo,
    Odle lady hee, idle leedle lady odle hoo.
    Idle leedle lady, odle leedle lady,
    Idle leedle lady odle lady hoo,
    A yodel o- - -dle lady, idle leedle lady odle hoo.

"Cowboy Buckaroo" by Mason Williams

West that is starkly at odds with reality. The actual work involved in being a cowboy was dirty and low paid. While cowboys often were very proficient at their work, they had a very specific skill set that was not easily transferable. Literacy was not a requirement, and so a significant number of cowboys were African-American and Hispanic. Theirs was hard work that held little nobility—they gathered cattle on the open range and brought them to the ranch, and finally drove them to a distant railhead for shipment to processors. The cattle drive, though storied, was a rather short-lived aspect of Western life, since it lasted only until the railroads became more accessible.

Nevertheless, the cowboy became "America's Knight in Shining Armor." He embodied the independent unfettered loner bound only by his own rules and ethical code of conduct, and came to stand as a model for certain types of behavior. The dime novels of the late nineteenth century first made this image popular, and this genre continues to exist in the twenty-first century. It has taken various forms, but the honest man or small group of men standing up to corruption against great odds is an American archetype that found its most popular incarnation with the cowboy.

America's fascination with the West was building at a time when the frontier was rapidly disappearing. In 1890 the Census Bureau announced that there was nowhere in the United States that had the sparse settlement that was the definition of the term *frontier*. In 1893 historian Frederick Jackson Turner postulated his "Frontier Thesis." In it he said that the process of settling the West was an essential part of the American story which was deeply embedded in the American character. America was becoming increasingly urban and the days of the "Wild West" were effectively over. Yet, the late nineteenth century saw the increasing popularity of Buffalo Bill's Wild West Show, and plays and books about the glory of the West. While the actual frontier West was fading into history, the imagined one was growing exponentially.

Real working cowboys had had a significant singing culture. They sang for their own amusement and, more pragmatically, as a way to keep their cattle calm. Famed ethnomusicologist John Lomax's *Cowboy Songs and Other Frontier Ballads* was published in 1910 and was the first scholarly collection of these memorable songs. His work and those of other collectors are a key source for the preservation of this genre of music. Records and radio grew the audience for cowboy music through the 1920s as they had previously done for hillbilly and blues.

The Great Depression slowed, but did not stop, the development of new music and musical innovation. Western music continued to be made and a new technology brought a new musical hero to American culture—one that would embody an American heroic archetype and put a guitar in his hands.

When *sound* was added to motion pictures, starting with *The Jazz Singer* in 1927, a new avenue was developed for the spread of music and musical tastes. Like records and radio, movies were dominated by the big band and swing sounds of the era. There was, however, one movie creation that would change the look and feel of country music—the singing cowboy. Carson Robison and Vernon Dalhart were two very popular singers of the era who performed cowboy music which predated and perhaps anticipated this stereotype. Not only did these heroes of the screen introduce many Americans to "Western" music, but they also introduced cowboy fashion to country music. Many of these tunes were modern compositions, not those of the traditional cowboy, but that did not diminish the feel, look, and spirit of the music. These screen cow punchers often accompanied themselves with guitars, and many of their fans wanted to sound and look like their favorite cowboy stars.

Gene Autry Songbook

The screen brought the cowboy image to life. Gene Autry and Roy Rogers were only two of many who portrayed the wholesome image of the cowpuncher. The two men had both been singers before they became movie stars. Autry had sung on radio and records, often emulating Jimmie Rodgers, while Roy Rogers began his singing career as a member of the seminally important Western group "The Sons of the

186. I'M BOUND TO FOLLOW THE LONGHORN COWS

FROM: p. 19 of *Cowboy Songs*, Lomax (Macmillan, N.Y., 1910, 1938). Arranged by Alec Moore, ex-cowpuncher of Austin, Texas, and by J. and A. Lomax.

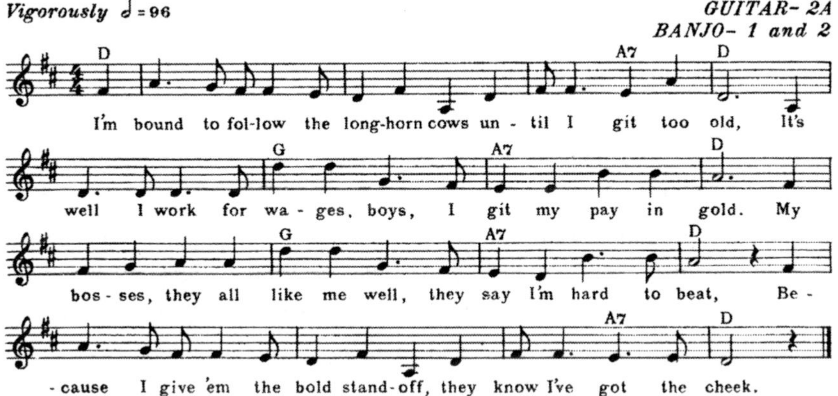

1 I'm bound to follow the longhorn cows until I git too old,
It's well I work for wages, boys, I git my pay in gold.
My bosses, they all like me well, they say I'm hard to beat,
Because I give 'em the bold stand-off, they know I've got the cheek.

2 Yes, I'm a rowdy cowboy, just off the stormy plains,
My trade is cinchin' saddles and pullin' bridle reins,
O I can tip the lasso, boys, it is with graceful ease,
I can rope a streak of lightnin' and ride it where I please.

3 Now when we git them bedded down, we think it's for the night,
Some horse will shake a saddle and give the herd a fright,
The herd will rise up to its feet and madly dash away,
'It's movin' time, to the lead, my boys,' you'll hear some cowboy say.

4 And when we git them rounded up and just about quieted down,
The storm's a-risin' in the west, and fire plays on their horns,
The foreman says, 'Stay with 'em, boys, your pay will be in gold'—
I'm bound to follow the longhorn cows, until I git too old.

5 One night way up in Kansas, I had a pleasant dream,
I dreamed I'se back in Texas, boys, down by some pleasant stream,
My love was right beside me, boys, she'd come to go my bail,
But I woke up broken-hearted with a yearling by the tail.

6 Now if I had a little stake, I soon would married be,
But another week and I must go, the boss said so today.
My girl must cheer up courage and choose some other one,
For I'm bound to follow the longhorn cows until my race is run.

Collected by Alan Lomax

Pioneers," whose skillful harmonies and arrangements helped define the genre. As cowboy stars, Autry, Rogers, and the rest always stood for what was right and lived by a code of chivalry that was no less well-defined than that of King Arthur's Roundtable. They also could sing like birds and play a mean guitar. Doug Green, in his book *Singing in the Saddle* points out that screen cowboys rarely if ever had anything to do with cows. There were dozens of singing cowboys who were able to dress in white and fight the bad guys in violent scuffles while somehow never getting mussed up. Irony abounds in such portrayals.

Gene Autry's official rules of cowboy conduct said that "… a cowboy must not take unfair advantage of an enemy; must never go back on his word; must always tell the truth; must be gentle with children, elderly people, and animals; must not possess racially or religiously intolerant ideas; must help people in distress; must be a good worker; and must respect women, his parents and the nation's laws." This is a remarkable set of rules and also a code for living that underscores individual responsibility. It is no wonder that Mason Williams, during his testimony, pointed to cowboy heroes as contributory to a youth movement that couched its fervor for change in exactly these terms.

One of the interesting aspects of the guitar industry is that there is sometimes little correlation between innovation in the instrument and its popularity, and thus sales. Nowhere was this truer than with the sales of guitars that were propelled by the singing cowboy. Western artists did not ask a guitar to do anything different than what guitars of the time already did, so the designs stayed fundamentally the same. Rodgers played both archtops and flat tops while the majority of his peers played only flat tops. Like automobiles, occasional changes in the appearance of guitars were important for their sales, and this concept introduced a new look to the instruments.

The impact of the "cowboy look" was felt throughout the guitar industry. Some guitars, most notably the Gibson J- 200, were designed to appeal to Western players, and so they had Western decorative themes. They became, in essence, part of the stage costume. The first J-200 was, as best we know, built for cowboy star Ray Whitley in 1937. This 17-inch jumbo guitar (or as it was referred to then as a "super jumbo" guitar), had an intricately carved bridge, a very fancy pick guard, and beautiful inlay work. It became a favorite choice of cowboy stars and later the country music artists who would adopt the cowboy *persona*.

Roy Rogers with prototype Martin OM-45

Gibson was not the only company appealing to this market. Martin, a company that had made elaborate guitars for decades, continued and expanded this tradition. The Martin 45 series, with its elaborate appointments, was played by several major cowboy stars. Gene Autry, who owned several J-200s, was the first owner of a Martin D-45. He also owned a beautiful 000-45, among other lavishly appointed instruments. The 45 series is Martin's most elaborate production guitar. Its abalone-bound body, neck, and other design details set it apart from other types. Martin's 45 series and Gibson's J-200 perfectly matched the ever-more-elaborate outfits that screen cowboys would

Ray Whitley

wear. The Gibson J-200s and Martin 45s produced prior to World War II are some of the most desirable flattop guitars ever made. Both series are still in production today.

The vast majority of cowboy theme guitars were not up to the usual Martin or Gibson quality. They were sold primarily through catalog sales from companies such as Sears, Montgomery Ward, and Simpsons in Canada. Montgomery Ward's "Recording King" series featured the Carson Robison and Ray Whitley models which were made by Gibson, although of lesser quality than guitars with the Gibson brand on them. In fact, most of the cowboy guitars of the period were not quality instruments. Harmony, Kay,

Ray Whitley Gibson

Gibson J-200

Regal and other manufacturers made low-cost and beginners' instruments out of wood. While limited, they were normally playable, and were enjoyed by many aspiring musicians.

By the 1950s wooden cowboy guitars were being phased out and replaced with those made of plastic or fiberboard. These were essentially toys. They may have some collectible value today but their worth is mainly as a novelty item or historical artifact, and they have no value as actual musical instruments. Some are still being made using the exact same techniques that were used in the 1950s.

No matter what they were constructed of, most low-cost cowboy guitars have characteristics in common. They are stenciled or, in the case of plastic, embossed with Western scenes, and often the names of movie or television heroes are emblazoned upon them. The Gene Autry "Melody Ranch," one of many Autry models, was a big seller, as were the Roy Rogers-branded instruments. The Lone Ranger, Hopalong Cassidy, and other cowboy celebrities had their own guitar models even though they ironically neither played nor sang in any of their movies.

Surely most of these guitars wound up in closets, the trash, or in yard sales. For many owners it would be their last engagement with a guitar, but for other people cowboy models were a stepping stone to better guitars and a lifelong passion for them. There are many reasons that people pick up a guitar. The folk boom, the Beatles era, the blues greats, and other trends have inspired people to play guitars. This is also true of the singing cowboy.

Starting in 1954 Gretsch made a series of cowboy-themed guitars, with the Roundup model being perhaps the most wildly Western design. Three of these were archtop electric guitars with "G" branding, horseshoe patterns on pick guards, and other Western appointments. The Rancher was the only flat top cowboy Gretsch. These were produced as the singing cowboy was on the wane, but the influence of cowboy music and style in country music had become obvious. The Gretsch models gradually lost their Western motif, and it was gone entirely by 1963.

The fashion statement is one of the longest-lasting impacts of the singing cowboy. While commercial cowboy music had long been seen as part of hillbilly or country music, the two had become tightly intertwined by the 1940s. It was then that *Billboard* dropped the name "hillbilly" and began to call the music "country-western." (Q: "What kind of music do you play?" A: "Both kinds—country and western.") From then on fancy western hats, boots, and clothing have become a staple of American country music. Little Jimmy Dickens, Porter Wagner, and Brad Paisley all had their take on how a country artist should dress on stage. Along with honky-tonks, Western wear shops are ubiquitous in country music havens such as lower Broadway in

Gene Autry "Melody Ranch" guitar

Nashville. It is fair to say that the rhinestone industry owes a debt to the movie cowboy that equals that of guitar producers.

The fascination with the West is not strictly an American phenomenon. It is global. Katy Moffatt, a touring country and Americana artist since

Gretsch Roundup

the 1970s, has a cowboy hat in her closet. It was needed, she says, for a country music tour of Indonesia that she played in 1991. You can still see country performers throughout Europe and Asia dressed in cowboy hats and boots. In post-World War II Germany, replicas of Western towns were built where people would dress in Western garb and spend the day in the German equivalent of Tombstone, Arizona.

While the singing cowboy movies lost popularity in the decades after World War II, the fascination with the West did not. Television in the 1950s was rife with cowboy shows. Some, like Roy Rogers or the Lone Ranger, were geared toward children, but others, such as *Have Gun Will Travel*, *Gunsmoke*, *Sugarfoot*, *Bonanza* and others, were prime time "horse operas" that were not to be missed. The message was the same as those of the Western movies—stand up for the right. Their distinctive TV theme songs continue to resonate through the minds of an entire generation.

It is always difficult to speculate about how and why something becomes significant in popular culture. Yet the great contradictions of the immediate post-World War II era seem to point in several directions. The United States had emerged from World War II as one of two dominant "superpowers" on the planet. The country was at the top of the economic food chain and was ushering in a vast expansion of the middle class, education, and consumer culture. At the same time, there was a great fear of the Soviet Union and its

"Don't Fence Me In" recorded by Gene Autry

communist ideology that was only exacerbated when the Soviets obtained nuclear capability.

America had embraced the Western image in the late nineteenth century as it was becoming more urban and rapidly losing its innocence; it further embraced Western culture in the 1940s and '50s as it engaged in a political, economic, and social duel with the Soviet Union. The common element was rapid disorienting change. In both cases, a romanticized past offered escape, and perhaps solace, from an uncertain present. One of the most discernible differences between the capitalism and democracy of the United States and the Communist ideology of the Soviet Union was the role of the individual. There is no greater symbol of that individuality than the romanticized cowboy.

The singing cowboy's dominance may be gone but his impact lives on. Just watch Little Jimmy Dickens in his spangled Western suit playing his giant J-200 to realize that the ghosts of Gene Autry, Roy Rogers, and Ray Whitley still prowl the earth. Guitars may not have made giant leaps in acoustic properties or fundamental design to accommodate cowboy music, but they were beautifully artful and uniquely American. They remain an important reminder of who Americans wanted to be.

CHAPTER SIX

Breaking Down Walls

Race has consistently been one of the most difficult issues in American history. It was the elephant in the room at the Constitutional Convention of 1787, and had been a central cause of confusion and conflict before the convention. It has remained so ever since. The issue of race has been made more difficult in America because of the nation's founding ideal of individual rights and liberty.

How could a nation justify slavery at the same time that it committed itself to liberty? The answer was to make slavery race-based. It was not simply a status one was born into, or the result of capture in war, as it had been in other times and places. It was, instead, based on national origin and skin color. Slaves were black and the justification of depriving them of liberty was that they were not fully human. That belief has made the issue a complicated one.

There was one significant area where cultures and people both white and black mingled. That was music. From the earliest days of British settlement and the slavery that eventually accompanied it, African rhythms combined with British traditional music to create uniquely American forms of music. This was not by design and was certainly not an effort toward equality or racial mixing; it was simply a fact of life.

One of the earliest and most visible aspects of this is seen in the wide adoption of the banjo—an instrument imported from Africa. First made with gourds, it was not until later that it took the shape that we know today. The banjo is an excellent medium to meld different musical traditions, since it is both melodic and percussive.

Blacks and whites rarely played music together in dance halls or minstrel shows, even though musical styles were crossing racial lines. The South, with its large slave population, was a fertile ground for the transmission of musical themes. Both races were exposed to the music of the other, and without conscious thought or design the process of amalgamation began.

The minstrel show was an odd form of racially-based entertainment that was wildly popular throughout America in the nineteenth and early part of the twentieth century. In these performances whites would apply blackface and play banjo music, punctuated with what can only be described as racist humor. These shows would reinforce the stereotypes that whites had of African-Americans. Interestingly, and against modern stereotypes, minstrelsy originated and was very popular in northern states. During this period the banjo was largely abandoned by the black community. It receded to such a point that people today are surprised when the African-American string band "The Carolina Chocolate Drops" plays traditional "Old Time" music and rightfully claim it as their own.

The Harlem Renaissance of the 1920s was an explosion of art, including poetry, painting, and music. Here jazz came into full flower. The Cotton Club brought whites into Harlem to hear Duke Ellington, Bessie Smith, Billie Holiday, Louis Armstrong, and Jelly Roll Morton, among others. These performers played a new syncopated music that had been born in Africa, transformed in the southern states, and brought north in the great migration of African-Americans after the Civil War.

Music broke down the barriers between races in other ways. In 1935 *Porgy and Bess* opened on Broadway and four years later the great African-American opera singer Marian Anderson performed on Easter Sunday on the Capitol Mall. But barriers were still tall. When the celebrated white guitarist Eddie Lang played with black artists he did so using a pseudonym.

After being encouraged by Columbia producer John Hammond, Benny Goodman broke through more barriers when he added African-American guitarist Charlie Christian to The Benny Goodman Sextet in 1939. Christian popularized the electric guitar and his stint with Goodman served to both legitimize the instrument and the artist himself. Apparently Goodman lost some gigs because of his inclusion of Christian, but said it was a price he was able and willing to pay.

Minstrel performer

This was merely the first wave of the cross pollination that would so heavily impact American culture later in the twentieth century. It was the blues, and its children—jazz and rock—which would redefine American music. As the great Muddy Waters said, "The Blues had a baby and they called it Rock and Roll." Guitar makers both reflected this reality and propelled it forward. Instruments would change, but, just as importantly, change would come in the way instruments were marketed and sold.

While the merchandising for some items such as records was racially targeted, guitars were not. Record labels typically concentrated their efforts in recording for various well-defined markets. Hillbilly music, later to be called country, was one market, and "race records" was another. The latter were blues and gospel recordings which targeted the African-American audience.

Guitar and banjo makers did not produce specific instruments for different market segments based on anything other than cost. A guitar did not have to be made a certain way to play either black or white music. Manufacturers in both New York and Chicago made instruments geared toward lower income Americans of all races, but they did not cross racial lines in either their advertizing or design.

For example, New York Band Instrument, the Gibson dealer in New York City, hosted two concerts to promote Gibson instruments in 1939. One featured all-white performers playing for a white audience while the other had black artists playing for black patrons. Music may have been building bridges, but many were not ready to cross it.

If it had been difficult for Americans to square the circle on racial issues at the time of the Constitutional Convention, that difficulty increased with the American experience during World War Two. When America entered the war in December of 1941, there was a bombardment of films, posters, radio, and other media to explain why this war had to be fought. Frank Capra's *Why We Fight*, a series of documentary films, was typical. It painted the war as a battle between light and dark, between good and evil, between liberty and slavery.

World War II was fought with a segregated American army, and the cognitive dissonance required to maintain segregation after the war became ever more difficult. The discovery of the Holocaust, the deliberate murder of six million Jews and at least four million other victims, was clear evidence

Charlie Christian

of where racism might lead. Americans were forced to look upon their own racism with new eyes.

Color lines began to fall, albeit slowly. In 1947 Jackie Robinson broke the color barrier and racial segregation in major league baseball. While many supported this move by the Brooklyn Dodgers, Robinson was met with massive amounts of racial hatred.

In 1948 President Harry Truman began the desegregation of the military. Again, this move was met with great hostility in some quarters. However, barriers continued to fall and many of them were based on music.

The final nails in the coffin of legally protected racism came in 1954 when the Supreme Court ruled that "separate but equal" was unconstitutional, followed in 1964 by the passage of the Civil Rights Act. While these were important steps, changing law is one thing—changing culture is quite another.

While whites and blacks had come together musically for generations, the 1950s saw an open, conscious, and significant popular exchange. Rock and roll came to define the new relationship between white and black culture. For some this was welcome, but for others it was horrifying. It was not just that white kids were cheering black performers. Certainly, that was part of the issue. Lines would form and white teenage girls would scream their delight at seeing and hearing Chuck Berry, Fats Domino, Little Richard, James Brown, and a slew of other African-American individual performers and groups.

But just as disconcerting was the fact that this new music was being performed by white musicians who had adopted the backbeat and sensuality of rock and roll. Sam Phillips, of Sun Records in Memphis, had once said that he could make a million dollars if he could find a white man who sounded black, and Elvis Presley was his answer. Although not the first to sing with a backbeat, Elvis brilliantly combined African-American, gospel, and country music into something that was new and completely accessible to American teenagers. Elvis brought sensuality into the open.

Many Americans did not know how to handle this new music. Elvis, Buddy Holly and Bill Haley were all opening doors that had never been opened before. Some gleefully walked through them while others tried to either slam them shut or modify the music so that it was more acceptable to conventional norms. It was the latter that got us Pat Boone's painful rendition of *Tootie Fruity*, Fabian, Frankie Avalon, and a slew of other white performers who produced an emasculated form of rock and roll.

Other members of the public reacted using violent means. Records were burned in barrels and run over by cars. Rock was called "the devil's music,"

Chuck Berry

"jungle music," and "nigger music." For these people, rock was a dangerous import that had its origins in the African-American community and was a threat to their children and the social stability of their world.

Guitar makers were uninterested in what color people were or whether the accent was on the backbeat. Their goal was to produce as many instruments as they could for anyone who wanted to buy them.

From the 1930s through the 1950s guitar companies made a wide array of instruments. They ranged from very expensive to very low end instruments often sold in catalogues. The images in guitar company advertising uniformly showed white people playing guitars. In the 1930s and '40s archtop guitars were seen as serious instruments, and photographs normally showed very well-dressed people playing them. Flat tops, on the other hand, were pictured with country artists. Catalogues such as Sears displayed instruments alone,

Elvis

and were thus racially neutral. African-Americans were nowhere to be seen, but this situation was about to change.

The combination of the folk boom, jazz, rock and roll, and changing racial norms in America that accompanied these styles was soon reflected in American guitar marketing. The catalogues of the Guild Guitar Company are illustrative of this trend. In 1961 the catalogue was all white, but by the mid-1960s Guild catalogs prominently featured African-American performers. By 1967 Richie Havens and George Benson were sharing a cover with the Smothers Brothers and Eric Clapton. In the same decade Barry Cornfield and Mississippi John Hurt joined two members of the Wagonmasters and two white models wearing evening clothes, playing solid bodies on Guild's full line catalogue.

Gibson "Galaxy of Stars"

Guild catalogue 1967

In its 1962 catalogue, Gibson featured its first black artist. One of the thirty-six players pictured in the "Galaxy of Stars" was Norman Brown, who played with the Mills Brothers. In 1964 African-American jazz artist Wes Montgomery was prominently featured playing an L-5 CES. He continued to be the focus of various Gibson ads and catalogues throughout the mid-1960s. Blues great B.B. King was a featured endorser by 1973. White players were also featured of course, including Barney Kessel, Johnny Smith, and Trini Lopez. Each had Gibson signature guitars that were well-promoted by the company.

This was a near revolutionary moment in American race relations. Companies believed that featuring black artists would sell guitars to affluent white consumers as well as African-Americans. The ads featuring black performers were not in media targeted to that community, but rather were for general circulation. This was a first—the idea that the featuring of black performers would not offend nearly as many potential buyers as it would convince them of the quality and desirability of a manufacturer's guitars.

Guitar manufacturers were at the leading edge of making use of African-Americans to sell their products to a broad racial base of consumers. It was really the first industry to do so. While Robinson had broken into the major leagues of baseball in 1947, soon to be followed by many other African-American players, sports equipment makers did not immediately begin cross-racial advertising. They certainly did not predate the manufacturers of guitars in this regard.

This underscores the unique role that music played in the racial revolution that took place in the United States in the middle of the last century. In sports or other physical activities the presence of African-Americans did not fundamentally change the activity. A baseball player of any race would still hit the ball in the same way. This was not so with music. Here, the amalgamation of African-American blues, boogie, jazz, and rock broadened the very scope of the music that was being played. Timing, phrasing, and subject matter all changed, but African-American musicians were not distinguished as much by race as by the music they played.

This use of African-American artists went even further when Ovation Guitars introduced a Josh White model in 1965. White was a well-known African-American artist who had been performing for many years. He had been a folk performer, a lounge singer, an actor, and an activist. He had also been tainted by the aggressive investigations of the McCarthy era. Yet a guitar endorsed by him was still seen as a viable marketing tool.

The young Josh White

This is all the more significant since Ovation was then a brand new company with a brand new idea. Their guitars did not have the traditional wooden backs and sides. Instead, they had a molded bowl constructed with a type of fiberglass material. It was a sign of the new times that such a company would turn to an African-American for their first signature instrument. Their wager on the efficacy of the Josh White model was magnified because the company had neither a stable of other endorsers nor a long history to fall back upon. Neither White's race nor his political activities were seen as an impediment to selling guitars.

Josh White Ovation publicity photo

Interestingly, neither Harmony nor Kay pictured any African-Americans in their catalogues throughout the 1960s. These makers, who specialized in low cost instruments, ignored much of the budget guitar market that lay among low income peoples of all colors. Instead, they focused their efforts on white middle class youth whose financial restraints were the product of their ages, not race or class. Harmony and Kay instruments were, however, the stock and trade in pawn shops which, along with catalogues, served as main distributors of inexpensive instruments in low income neighborhoods of all races.

A good deal of the public image of instruments and their use lay outside the control of the companies making guitars. By the 1950s television had become ubiquitous in American society. Here too color barriers were strongly enforced, but music was somewhat of an exception. Blacks and whites would not be seen playing together regularly for another decade, but black artists would appear on national television playing guitars made by Gibson, Fender, Epiphone, and others. Then as now, consumers linked the music they loved and the artists that played it with the instruments those performers used on stage.

The Ed Sullivan Show, which ran on CBS from 1948 until 1971, was a showcase and proving ground for many aspects of American entertainment. In addition to comedians, tumbling acts, and that really annoying mouse-thing puppet, music, in particular rock and roll and its cousins, played a prominent role. The Sullivan show was a must-see on Sunday evenings for many Americans, and inclusion on it was a stamp of acceptance. During its long run the show hosted a wide array of artists. Sullivan's laconic introductions often pointed to some of the most dramatic moments in

American musical history. Many of the artists were African-American. The Jackson Five, Stevie Wonder, the Supremes, Martha and the Vandellas, Fats Domino, James Brown, Bo Diddley, and a host of other important black musicians were featured throughout the run of the program.

The Sullivan show was a sign that a musical act had broad appeal and was, to some degree, welcome in American homes. White acts like the Beach Boys, the Beatles, Elvis, the Doors, and many others recognized that inclusion on Sullivan's variety show was a sign that they had arrived. For African-Americans, it was a signal that the artists and their music had gained acceptance.

Guitars were central to many rock and roll performers. The guitars that they played became objects of desire for any aspiring rock and roll star. Even though guitar companies may not have featured people like Chuck Berry in their advertisements in the 1960s, the presence of Berry and others on TV accelerated sales of the guitars they played.

The role of African-American music in the broad landscape of American popular music cannot be overemphasized. It is the very fabric of how we listen to and experience music. One musicologist has noted that when Canadian audiences clap along at a concert they hit the one and the three; Americans clap on the two and the four—the backbeat. That is, of course, a direct legacy of the rhythm imported to America from Africa, and it has become part of our musical DNA. Even Bluegrass, a music closely identified with white America, plays to the backbeat.

The guitar industry responded to changes in American culture, acknowledged them, and, in some ways propelled them. The use of African-American artists to sell instruments to the broad spectrum of American consumers was an affirmation that the walls were indeed coming down. As the biblical Joshua brought down the walls of Jericho with his trumpet, Chuck Berry chipped away at the wall of racial division with his Gibson ES-335.

CHAPTER SEVEN

The Folk Boom(let)

In 1958 a group consisting of three tidy college kids, the Kingston Trio, had a monster hit with *Tom Dooley*, a modern take on an old folk song from North Carolina. It told a story of love and murder—Tom's run for the Tennessee border, his subsequent capture, and the hangman's rope that took his life. The account was true to the original, but musically the Trio's version was without the rough edges, since it featured a bouncy melody and smooth harmonies. It was sanitized—in essence a folk song remake with pop sensibilities.

Without it there may have been no folk boom, and no significant expansion in the production of flat top guitars. The subsequent rise of popular folk music is both significant on its own and sets the stage for the epochal changes in the world of guitars that would soon follow it.

The Kingston Trio's *Tom Dooley* was not the first sanitized folk hit. The Weavers, led by Pete Seeger, who would become a folk icon, had preceded the young Trio with their hit song *Goodnight Irene*, but contentious politics would soon derail the blossoming success of the Weavers and other folk artists.

Folk music is part of any nation's experience. It is the music of many people over many years; the music that people played and sang for entertainment, worship, memory, and courtship. It is the peoples' music passed down through generations, with no transcriptions or copyrights. In America, folk music is also the amalgamation of musical genres that came from the diverse peoples who had settled in this country.

John Lomax began to collect these songs as a young man in Texas. He published *Cowboy Songs and other Frontier Ballads* (with an introduction by

Tombstone of Laura Foster whose murder by Tom Dula inspired the song "Tom Dooley"

Theodore Roosevelt) in 1910. This was one of the first collected publications of American folk songs. Incidentally, compiling this collection helped to launch his and his son Alan's lifelong careers of cataloguing American folk music. Their work preserved and popularized folk music, from ballads to blues, and also led to the discovery of performers whose raw power would engage generations of Americans. Huddie Ledbetter (Lead Belly), for instance, stands out as one of the many artists popularized by the Lomaxes.

In the 1920s and '30s folk music came to be associated with social reform, the labor movement, and the Communist party. The Great Depression had raised many issues about American life and economics. Some people believed that a revolutionary approach was necessary to provide equity in our economic system. Radical movements on both the left and the right gained some favor in American politics, but compared to Europe, these movements were marginalized. Neither fascists on the right nor Communists on the left gained much traction in the American political system.

However, Communism did have an appeal to the labor movement, whose members believed that they had been dragged down by a capitalist system where the deck was often stacked against them. It was not uncommon for organizers and members to use songs to energize the movement and give a sense of community to it.

In particular, Woody Guthrie, the great Oklahoma singer, songwriter, and crusader, used his songs as tools for organization and social change. *This Land is Your Land*, *Union Maid*, *So Long It's Been Good to Know You*, and a host of other Guthrie songs were all written as forms of protest and affirmation for the dispossessed. He united with Pete Seeger, Lee Hayes and Millard Lampell to form the socially-active Almanac Singers between 1940 and 1943.

The Cold War that followed World War II led to a period of great suspicion in America. The late 1940s and early '50s were the days of the McCarthy hearings and other institutional attempts to root out Communism and its sympathizers, both real and imagined. A very wide swath was cut. Among others, folk artists were investigated, and some were blacklisted— without any trial or conviction they were banned from working in movies, television, and music. Pete Seeger was banned, Burl Ives was investigated, and Josh White's career was severely limited, while other folk singers had greatly truncated professional lives. There was a taint thrown on the whole genre, and folk songs and folk singers were pegged to left wing social revolution.

Tom Dooley was a reversal of this trend. This was not the raw folk music of Pete Seeger, Woody Guthrie, or Lead Belly, and it was certainly not the music of the Appalachian Mountains or the cotton fields of Mississippi. It was upbeat and close to cheerful, and was performed by neatly groomed college students. It was the music performed by cowboys, farmers, slaves, and prisoners that had been collected by John and Alan Lomax, but it was presented in a more innocent format.

Nineteen fifty-eight, the year of *Tom Dooley*, was a very odd time in the United States, with a mixture of pride, arrogance, and fear enveloping the country

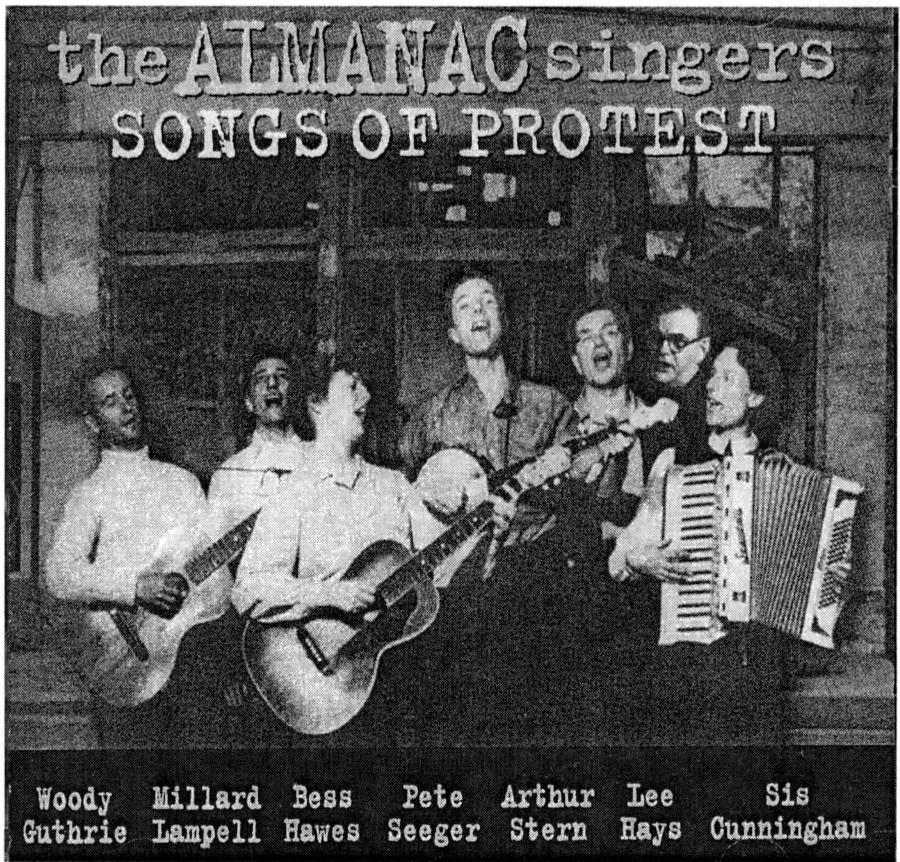

The Almanac Singers

Economically we were at the top of the food chain, and products made in the United States were the envy of the world. The miracle of quick and efficient production necessitated by World War II was sustained by pent up demand. It was a time of burgeoning economic prosperity, and many believed that the American way of life had proven itself to be the best of all possible worlds.

There was, however, a competing sense of anxiety. Once the sole nuclear power of the world, the United States had recently been joined by the Soviet Union in possessing these awesome weapons of destruction. Then, in October, 1957, the Soviets launched Sputnik, the first artificial satellite. This sent shivers down the spines of Americans. It was a great technological achievement, and it showed that the Soviet Union, with its Communist political and economic system, was also capable of great accomplishments.

Pete Seeger testifies to the House on Un-American Affairs Committee (HUAC)

The Kingston Trio

The military implications were stark. Sputnik itself was no threat; it was a small ball that circled the Earth and sent out harmless electronic beeps. It was the rocket that propelled the satellite into space that caused fear. A technology that could defeat the gravity of the Earth could also deploy weapons between continents. Such missile technology, married to nuclear weapons, was an Armageddon scenario. Americans began planning for civil defense and digging bomb shelters, while their children huddled under wooden desks in preparation for the coming Soviet nuclear attack.

It was against this background that America fell in love with the music of its past in its new clean-cut form. The Kingston Trio, the Brothers Four, the Limelighters, the Chad Mitchell Trio, the Highwaymen, Peter, Paul, and Mary, and others would sell millions of albums. The new/old music was a connection with the past, but was a tidied up version of the American experience. It was a way to link to American history in a way that removed some of the warts.

Lead Belly's *Cotton Fields*, a song depicting grueling hard work for very little reward, became a bouncy sing-along for people in small coffeehouses and rather swank nightclubs. Guthrie's *This Land Is Your Land*, written as a reply to what Guthrie perceived as the over-simplicity of *God Bless America*, would become a patriotic anthem sung by millions of schoolchildren. It still is.

Even the songs of grueling labor in the Caribbean became happy songs for middle class white Americans. Harry Belafonte's *Banana Boat Song*, a truly stark vision of low paid work, was ironically transformed into a snappy popular tune.

People did far more than just listen to this music. It was quite easy to play in its basic form. With three or four guitar chords and a snazzy shirt with a button down collar you too could be a folksinger. While this was clearly a distorted view of the American folk canon, it was an accessible entry point to the genre for millions of people.

There was an alternative folk movement taking hold at the same time. On college campuses and in folklore societies people were searching for a more authentic folk experience. Groups like the New Lost City Ramblers eschewed popular folk music and developed a small but influential following on the

Woody Guthrie

college circuit. College campuses provided the first venues outside the South for bluegrass. This period was what is often referred to as the "folk boom." It began in 1958 with *Tom Dooley* and ended sometime around 1963.

Guitar makers were delighted with this new interest in their products. Folk music's basic instrument was the flattop guitar (which has round sound holes, as opposed to the "f holes" of arch top guitars). Flattop guitars had been used in American music for many years, especially among blues and country singers. But after 1958 flattop guitars sales increased at a significant pace. Gibson guitars increased their production of flattops from 8,944 in 1958 to 11,510 in 1962. Guild guitars increased its production, although specific numbers are not available. Other companies soon followed suit.

Dave Van Ronk, "The Mayor of MacDougal Street"

Martin guitars were in many ways admired as the gold standard during the folk boom. Martin was then in a very small factory with limited production capability. In 1958 the company made 6,515 guitars and in 1962 that number was 6,087, a slight drop. Martin would not be able to meet its demand until the company expanded with the construction of a new factory in 1964. In the years of the folk boom Martin was backordered for an average of two years.

Mississippi John Hurt, who was rediscovered in the 1960s and became a major figure in the folk revival

That does not mean that Martin did not join other manufacturers in responding to the demands of newly-minted folk musicians. Martin began to make both twelve string guitars and two "New Yorker" models. The latter were twelve-frets-to-the-body, steel-string guitars with slotted headstocks and wide

Martin New Yorker

finger boards. They were patterned after the Martin nylon string guitar that Fred Hellerman of the Weavers played with silk and steel strings, and were advertized as dual use guitars—suitable for either nylon or steel strings.

Gibson introduced two models specifically manufactured for folk players. Both were wide-necked, steel-string, twelve-fret guitars that aimed to fill the same niche as the Martin New Yorkers, including the dual use claim. The company also made twelve string guitars in two body sizes.

In 1964 Guild Guitars introduced their "Dreadnought" series. These 16" square-shoulder guitars were very derivative of the Martin dreadnoughts. Guild also began to make a broader range of twelve string guitars than either Martin or Gibson. The Guild twelve-strings quickly gained a reputation for their tone and projection.

Even Fender, known for their expertise with solid body electrics, jumped into the flattop guitar business. Their instruments, with bolt-on necks and Fender's customary six-on-a-side headstock, never gained much traction, and they were soon abandoned (Fender has since re-entered the flattop market with Asian-made instruments and an American-made line that recreates their 1960s designs.) Harmony and Kay, America's two largest guitar manufacturers, made thousands upon thousands of flattop guitars to meet the demand for those who could not afford a Martin, Gibson, or Guild. Unfortunately, exact numbers are not available.

The growth in guitar sales engendered during the folk boom was significant and very welcome. It did not, however, outstrip most manufacturers' capabilities. This was a sustainable expansion.

By 1963 the clean cut folk image was on the wane. The activism at the core of folk music in the 1930s and '40s returned with the likes of Bob Dylan, Phil Ochs, Joan Baez, Tom Paxton, Buffy St. Marie, and a host of artists who again began to use music as a form of social protest. Every hot button issue of the day was addressed by these topical singer-songwriters. War, civil rights, the Cold War, conformity, workers' rights, and many other topics were popular subjects. Some of the songs offered hope and love, while others painted a desperate and desolate future.

There are several reasons for this change. The United States was being challenged with issues that had been on the back burner of American politics for generations. The Civil War had not settled the issue of race in America. In 1954 the United States Supreme Court held that "separate but equal" was an oxymoron, and was a concept that was illegal on its face.

America after World War II was in a time of constant preparation for the next war. At age eighteen all American men were required to register for the draft. The nation had a large standing army and an enormous defense establishment. The policy of containment of Communism was in full effect, and the United States stood ready to enforce it. We had fought a non-decisive war in Korea and a conflict was brewing in the former French colony of Vietnam.

For many, John F. Kennedy's presidency had been seen as a turning point, the dawn of a new optimism. But in November of 1963, President Kennedy was assassinated in Dallas, and many young people interpreted this as the beginning of an end to optimism. For many, the Kennedy presidency was a turning point. Its image of youth, vitality, and confidence had been destroyed by an assassin's bullets. Americans of many stripes felt a deep sense of personal loss.

All of this was set against a background where baby boomers were coming into their political own. This group, born between 1946 and 1964, was, by and large, well-educated, privileged, and infused with the sense of its own power. Many of its members believed that it was their responsibility to create a new world while simultaneously correcting the injustices of the old. As Bob Dylan sang in *The Times They Are A-Changin'*: "Please get out of the new one if you can't lend your hand."

Peter, Paul, and Mary at the 1963 March on Washington for Jobs and Freedom.

At the same time new instrumentation was being added to music, and folk rock came into being. Drums and electric guitars erected the bridge that connected the songs of folk singers with rock and roll. It was not always an easy connection. Folk audiences rebelled when Bob Dylan plugged in and was backed by the Paul Butterfield Blues Band at the Newport Folk Festival in 1965. That same year the Byrds had a major folk-rock hit with Dylan's *Mr. Tambourine Man.*

The reluctance of some to accept this new incarnation of folk music did not slow down its mass appeal. Solid body, semi-solid body, and electric twelve-string guitars surged in popularity. Folk and rock's musical child expanded the demand for instruments beyond the flattop guitar.

The Byrds, the Mamas and the Papas, The Band, Crosby, Stills, Nash, and Young, and similar groups took to stages and the airwaves with a unique message and sound. This was the mid-1960s, and baby boomers, suddenly possessed with a sense of their own power and rightness, had a soundtrack.

Folk music, folk rock, and virtually every other form of popular music was about to be overshadowed. The next musical wave, combined with the earlier demand for guitars, would increase the popularity of these instruments to unimaginable heights. The demand and production of American guitars would triple from approximately 400,000 in 1962 to about 1.3 million by 1967.

The Beatles and the wave of British bands that followed them made guitars an essential part of youth culture. That process, begun with rock and roll and built upon by folk and folk rock, accelerated like a rocket. The demand overwhelmed the capacity of American manufacturers, even though they went into overdrive in an attempt to meet it. At the same time, large non-music related companies came to believe that there were easy profits to be made in the guitar business. A period characterized by poor design, poor workmanship, and declining profits, plus the demise of Harmony and Kay, and the near destruction of two of the nation's iconic guitar brands, would soon follow.

CHAPTER EIGHT

Be Careful Where You Step: The Rise and Fall of Corporate Giants

The 1960s witnessed an explosive growth in the popularity of guitars. In 1962 there were approximately 400,000 made in the United States; by 1965 that number had increased to about 1,300,000. This rise in production was caused by a number of factors, but chief among them was a British group that first performed on the Ed Sullivan Show—the Beatles. There were other bands that featured guitars and became popular, such as the Beach Boys, the Ventures, the Rolling Stones, and many more. But it was the Beatles that really lit the fuse that propelled the increase in guitar sales.

The resulting explosion led to a plethora of changes that took place in the realm of guitar manufacturing and production. Most notable among these changes was the increase in sales. With the onset of higher numbers throughout the 1960s, companies from outside the smallish world of guitar and musical instrument production came to realize that there were profits available in the manufacturer of guitars—*big* profits!

CBS believed that Fender would be a good fit for their music and entertainment business. They bought the California company in 1965 and infused it with a novel and unique philosophy. Chicago Musical Instruments (CMI), which was the parent company of Gibson, was bought by the Norlin Corporation in 1969. Norlin was a division of an Ecuadorian brewing company. The Guild Guitar Company, another American brand, was a relative newcomer to the industry, since it had only been founded in 1952. In 1966 it was purchased by Avnet, a company with broad business interests.

This was an era of conglomeration throughout much of American business, but nowhere was the impact felt more strongly than in the guitar universe.

This was certainly the case of Gibson and Fender, where the change of ownership and attitude was palpable. Leo Fender, while not a musician, had held musicians in the highest regard and had looked to them for guidance when designing guitars and amplifiers. From his earliest days he was fixated on making instruments of high quality while still maintaining a high profit margin. The new regime at Fender was neither composed up of musicians nor people truly committed to the manufacture of quality musical instruments. Management decisions were made by corporate executives who were neither knowledgeable of, nor committed to, the production of guitars.

At Gibson, M.I. Berlin, who had been the founder and chief executive at CMI, left the company almost immediately after its hostile takeover by Norlin. His son, Arnold "Arnie" Berlin, remained CEO of the instrument division of Norlin for six years. In a 2003 interview he said that the new management had no interest in what he and his father had considered a "lovely little company." Their goal was to grow the company and to grow its profits. Neither the words "lovely" nor "little" were part of their corporate vocabulary.

Leo Fender

The younger Berlin said that he was looked upon as someone who was simply opposed to change, but he insisted that this was not the case during his tenure. Instead, he was trying to prevent changes that would do harm to the product and the reputation of the company.

It would be wrong to conclude that Gibson went from the finest instruments to very bad ones at the moment of the Norlin acquisition, since this was not the case. Gibson quality had been on a downward curve throughout much of the 1960s. Stan Rendell, who taken over the presidency of

Gibson from legendary Ted McCarty, put several design changes and cost cutting measures into place. Some of these were beneficial but others, while improving efficiency, had not improved the quality of Gibson guitars.

Guitar sales continued to grow throughout the 1960s and into the early '70s, and it looked as if CBS, Norlin, and Avnet had made astute business decisions. That all came to a screaming halt after 1973, a period that witnessed a challenge to many aspects of the American economy and politics. In that year another Arab-Israeli war had broken out, and this soon led to an oil embargo by OPEC, with a resulting steep rise in gasoline prices throughout the United States. Long gas lines became the norm, and prices rose so quickly that pumps could not accommodate them when they shot up into three digits. This was part of a long period of inflation, and when combined with a stagnant fiscal environment, it created a challenging time throughout the American economy.

The United States was also in an era of political unrest. The very tumultuous end of the Vietnam War and the almost paralytic Watergate crisis, which led to the resignation of Richard Nixon, were fuel on a fire of uncertainty and doubt.

Since 1945 the United States had clearly been at the top of the economic food chain in the Western world. Europe and Japan had been devastated by the Second World War, and it took several decades for them to rebuild their economic base. In much of American business and industry there was a belief that America's dominant position was permanent and immutable, but a change would soon take place in global economics.

By the 1970s Europe and Japan had both recovered sufficiently, and had begun making products that would be competitive in American as well as other global markets. At first Japanese products were greeted with derision. "No one will buy those rice burners," was a phrase often repeated when Japanese automobiles were first introduced into the United States. But GM, Ford, and Chrysler changed their tune, because "Made in Japan" soon came to be viewed as a hallmark of value and quality, and not a source of ridicule. This arrogance in many areas of American business also carried over to the guitar industry. Many believed in American dominance as a matter of faith. Their dismissal of foreign competition would prove to be a great error.

Gas lines became common

The 1970s through the mid-80s saw a broad decline in the quality of American products. This is generally acknowledged throughout the guitar industry, but is difficult to quantify. In the automobile industry, on the other hand, a waning of quality was measurable. In 1980 only five of the thirteen automobiles rated positively by *Consumer Reports* were American-made, while seven of the ten rated "unreliable" were also American-made. The German company Mercedes topped the reliability list, and five Japanese manufacturers took up the remaining seven spots.

American guitar companies, too, began to see increased competition from international manufacturers, particularly from those in Japan. Yamaha made significant inroads into American acoustic guitar markets in the late 1960s that continued into the '70s. Their FG series of instruments provided a well-made, low-cost alternative flattop guitar comparable to those of American companies that had formerly dominated the introductory market. Harmony and Kay, two American companies that had produced thousands of instruments for decades, proved to be no match for the onslaught of Asian imports. Kay went out of business in 1969, and Harmony followed just six years later.

Japanese companies did not restrict themselves to the introductory market. Tokai, Yari, Alvarez, Takamine, and Ibanez were brand names of instruments made in Japanese factories. Some were high-quality copies of Martin, Guild, Gibson, and Fender guitars. These instruments compared well with their American counterparts and often offered great values. Those imported into the United States were more limited than the Japanese instruments sold in Japan and Europe. Many of these were of very high quality and were not geared for the introductory market. This trend continued to grow throughout the '70s and '80s and created a true global marketplace for both the production and the sale of fretted instruments.

The guitar industry was beset with another, and quite unique, problem. Musical tastes changed radically. In 1965 nine out of the top ten hits on the "Billboard Hot 100" featured music that had a preponderance of guitars at the forefront. Ten years later that same list contained only four hits that featured guitars. This was the era of disco, and guitars generally receded into the background of American popular music.

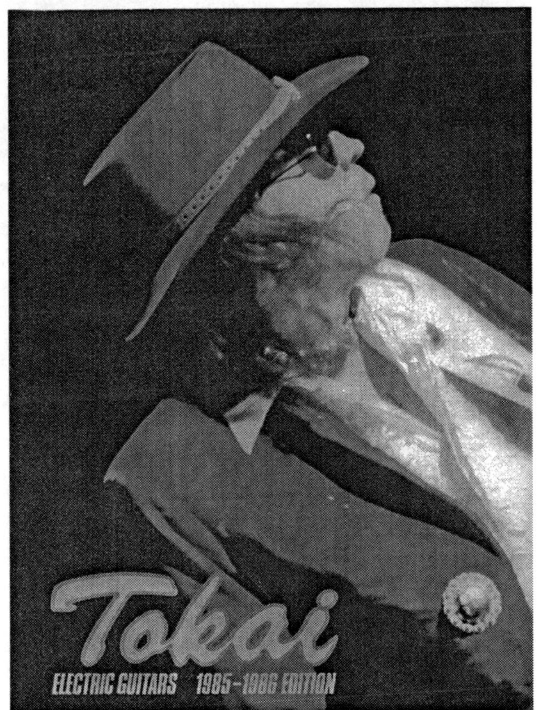

Stevie Ray Vaughn on a mid-1980s Tokai catalogue

There was one bright spot for guitar makers, but one in which the traditional American guitar companies were largely bypassed. Heavy metal had become popular, but Gibson, Fender, and Guild were unable to capitalize on this market. They made several attempts to do so, with Fender making the heavy metal Stratocaster and Guild making a series of guitars with pointed head stocks and bodies, but none of these sold in significant numbers. New companies like Jackson, Charvelle, and Kramer were favored by the younger players who wanted different features and were in no way enamored with designs that had been perfected in the 1950s, the staples at Fender and Gibson.

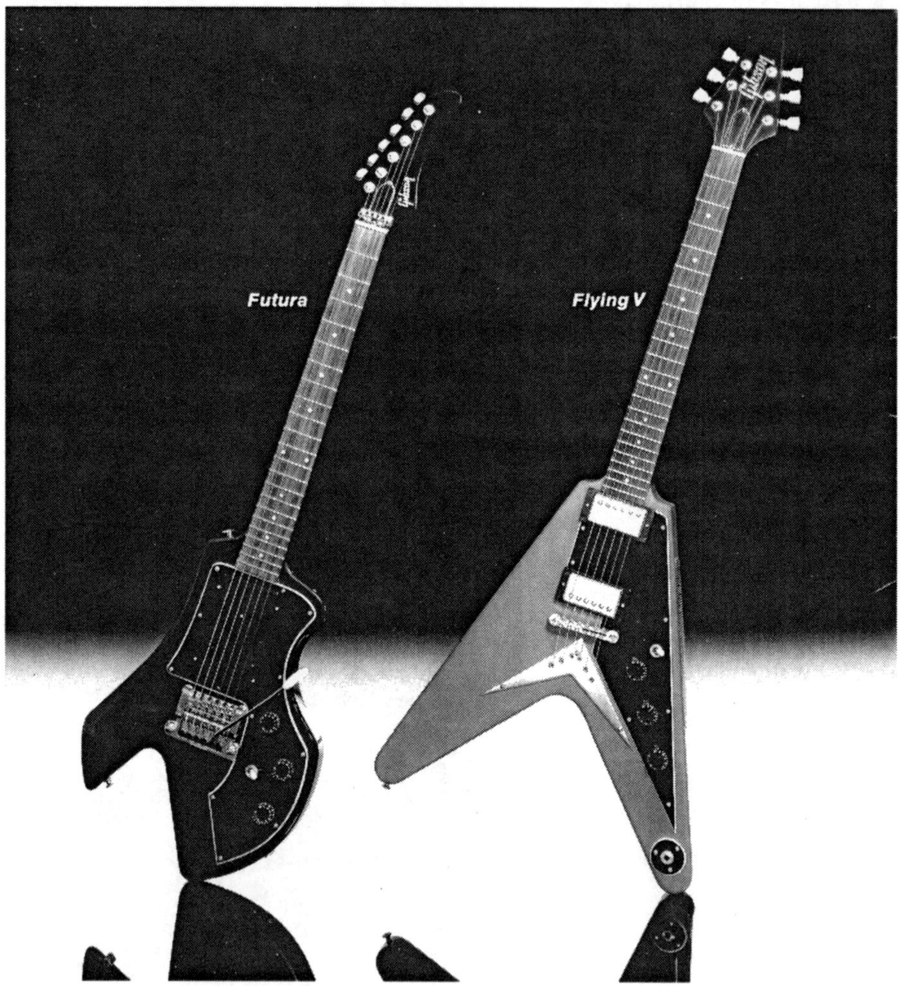

Gibson Flying V and Futura

The guitar industry was also challenged by demographic shifts. Baby boomers had been a significant part of the market but they dropped out when they began having children and their interests turned to things other than making music. They would reenter the market and help to rejuvenate it in the late 1980s, but their absence for a decade played havoc with the industry.

While sales of all guitars dropped, the market for flattop guitars fell off a cliff. Until about 1976 this market had been somewhat sustained through the popularity of folk rock. Leaders in that style, such as Crosby, Stills, Nash and Young, had been instrumental in maintaining sales of both new and vintage flattops. George Gruhn, a well-regarded expert on guitars and the guitar market, says that by the end of 1976 it was as if someone had simply turned off the switch. Martin, for example, made only 3,153 guitars in 1982, a remarkably low number for them.

All American guitar companies were having a hard time, but those owned by larger organizations had a compounded problem that was unique to their corporate position. Their parent companies had bought profitable guitar manufacturing enterprises and had expected those companies to maintain profitability even in this radically changed musical and economic environment. The inability of corporate managers to recognize some of the unique aspects of the guitar business added to their difficulties.

American guitar companies responded with a variety of new policies, cost-cutting measures, and fresh models in an attempt to survive in this highly competitive market. Gibson was perhaps the most aggressive. It introduced a variety of new solid body models—the RD, the L6-S, the L5-S, and the Firebrand series, as well as a new scientifically designed flattop series. The latter, the Mark Series guitars, were intended to showcase Gibson as an innovator so that it could reclaim its reputation for quality in acoustic guitars. The Mark Series guitars were designed with a great deal of technological innovation but, according to Bruce Bolen, who was in charge of the product, the quality of the handmade prototype could not be maintained when they went into production.

Gibson worked to cut costs in both manufacturing and warranty repairs. An example of the first is found in the specifications for the Gibson humbucking pickup. This pickup had been pioneered by Gibson, and was central to the sound for Gibson Les Pauls and ES 335s. Tim Shaw, a well-known guitar designer for Gibson and later Fender, was asked to reengineer the humbucking pickup, which had deviated from the specifications of its origin. The magnet wire that was being used caused a particular problem. Not only had the gauge of the wire been changed, but the coating on the wire had at some point been switched from the earlier enamel to polyurethane. Shaw wanted the gauge and the coating to be restored to their earlier specifications. The change of gauge would not raise costs so the earlier one was restored. The enamel wire, on the other hand, would cost one dollar more per pound and so was disallowed by Gibson management. One pound of wire makes dozens of pickups so the cost was miniscule. In the cost control mindset of management it was, however, too much.

The issue of warranty repairs had its most dramatic impact on Gibson's flattop guitars. Here is an issue that is unique to guitar manufacturing. Acoustic guitars have a built-in contradiction in their design and construction. Their sound is produced when the vibration of the strings is transmitted to the top of the guitar. For the best sound, the top and the other parts in that vibration chain, the saddle and bridge plate, have to vibrate freely. The problem is that strings exert a significant amount of tension that is, in effect, trying to pull the guitar part. Medium gauge acoustic strings, for example, have approximately 183 pounds of tension. So for a guitar to sound good it has to be built lightly, but if it is built too lightly, it will literally pull itself apart.

The company's concern with warranty repairs led to a decision to build guitars with thicker tops and heavier bracing. They also introduced "the double X brace," which was supposed to provide increased stability and not be detrimental to tone or volume. These supposed innovations led to new problems, most notably with gluing and finishes, which did not decrease warranty repairs. At the same time, they destroyed the sound of Gibson flattops.

Earlier Gibsons and Martins, as well as the guitars of other manufacturers, proved that guitars could be built so that they both stayed together and sounded good. To do so, however, requires a great deal of time and skill, which translates to cost. As a corporation, Gibson did not look back to its earlier eras. Instead they concentrated their efforts on making instruments that were innovative, but soon they and others like them would learn that their past was the repository of future success.

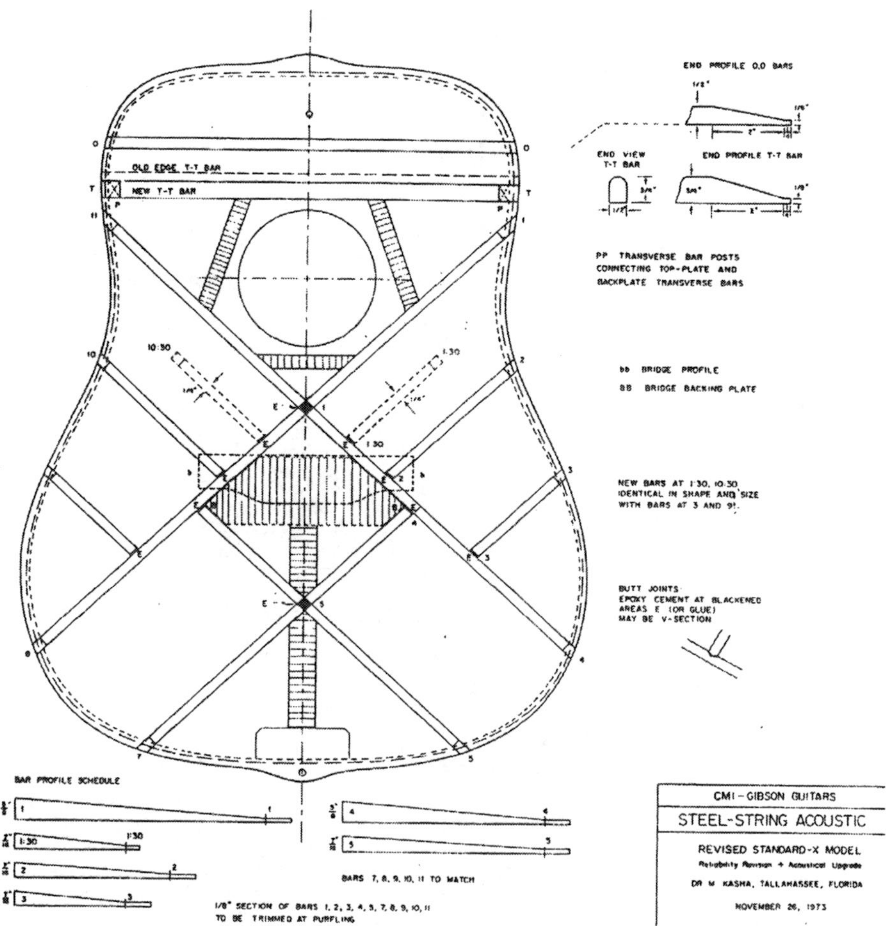

Gibson double X brace

Guild, also owned by a conglomerate, beefed up their flattops during 1972 for the same reason. The changes were not nearly as drastic as those at Gibson, and there are some modern buyers who prefer the sound of the 1970-1980s Guilds over those of later models. Guild was in a somewhat different position than Gibson and Fender. While owned by the Avnet Company, the person in charge of Guild for the majority of these years was Mark Dronge, son of Guild's founder Al Dronge. The younger Mr. Dronge was committed to the company as a family legacy and had a passion to make it successful. Avnet also took a more hands-off approach than did the owners of Gibson and Fender, which to some extent allowed Guild more freedom to operate.

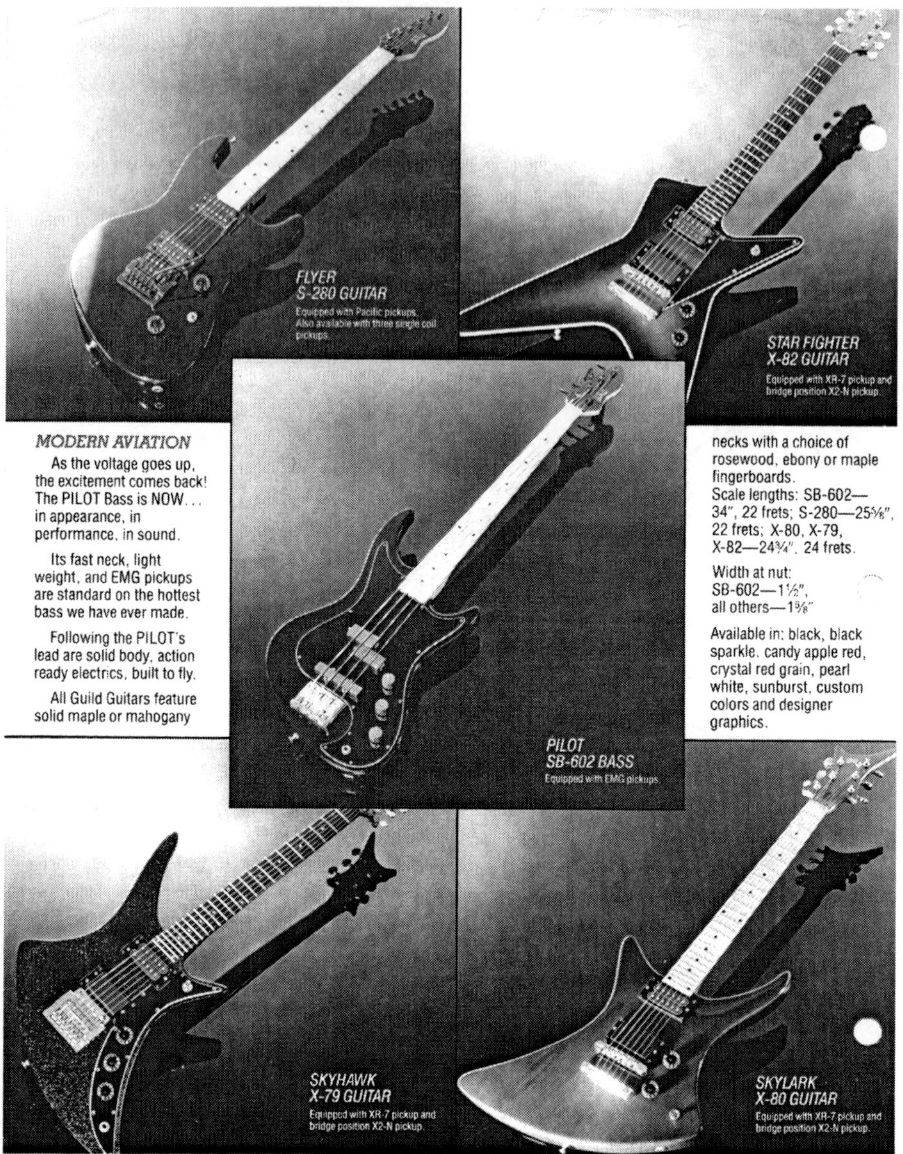

Guild made several models for the metal market with limited success

Gretsch had been sold to the Baldwin Piano and Organ Company when Fred Gretsch retired in 1967, since Baldwin had decided to broaden into other musical instruments. The company had earlier purchased the British guitar manufacturer, Burns, and had acquired Ode Banjos in 1967. There had been an earlier boom in Gretsch sales when the company's instruments were prominently used by both the Beatles and the Monkees.

Lucien Wulsin, Baldwin's president from 1964 through 1980, was in charge during this expansion, but he soon turned his interests to financial services. Earlier, Gretsch had become the guitar division, and later it would encompass all of Baldwin's instrument division. Gretsch guitar production was moved, and management, but not ownership, went through several changes. The line suffered from the same fluctuations in market forces as others, and experienced two factory fires in 1973. Its production was very uneven, and the line was out of production for a time in the late 1970s. It was returned to Gretsch family ownership in 1985.

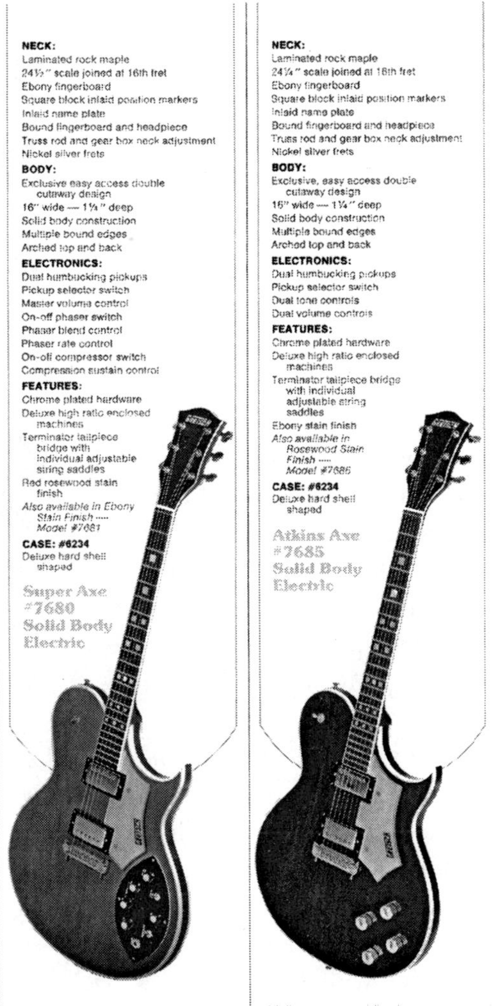

Gretsch from the Baldwin era

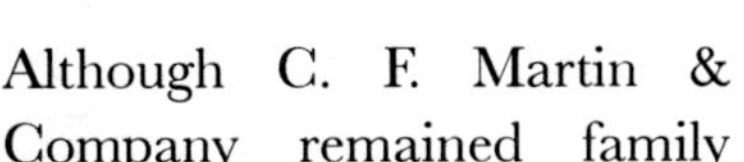

Although C. F. Martin & Company remained family owned, it also faced troubles during the same period. The company had increased production in 1968, when it opened a new factory, but soon had to deal with the declining sales of the 1970s and '80s. They also suffered from what one Martin employee of the time described as "a general lack of attention." Quality control was lax and certain changes were made to decrease warranty repairs. Martin tops and bracing did not become significantly heavier, but they did switch from a small maple to a large rosewood bridge plate in 1969, a modification which negatively impacted the sound of the guitars. In addition, Martin had a workers' strike in 1979 which lasted for nine months.

Fender had largely abandoned acoustic guitar production, but was also driven to cut costs and retain profit in their core solid body market under the CBS regime. Pickup wire once again became an easy target, since the purchasing department had found a pickup wire that was less expensive. While it was soon discovered that it was not appropriate for making Fender pickups, it was nevertheless purchased and used. This is but one example of inappropriate cost-cutting that took place at Fender. By the end of the 1970s it was quite clear to consumers that the quality of Fender products were not up to the company's earlier standards.

Fender Bronco

The situation went beyond pickups. Body shapes were changed to accommodate the limits of tooling, and the three-bolt neck replaced the traditional four-bolt. While there is nothing inherently defective with that design, it was manufactured badly and the guitars with the Fender three-bolt neck soon garnered a reputation for instability.

Fender also introduced new models, both to expand their product line and to offer a cheaper product. The Starcaster was a radical departure for Fender since it was a semi-hollow body guitar with humbucking pickups. The Bronco, on the other hand, was just a stripped-down solid body made to sell at a lower price point and thus compete with the imports. This was also true of the two-knob Stratocaster of 1982.

The Fender Swinger was made from unused 12 string parts

Dan Smith, who would later join Fender and be instrumental in its resurrection, was in charge of marketing for Yamaha Guitars in the 1970s. In a 2013 interview he said that as he visited retail dealers around the world as a representative of Yamaha he was often shown the poor quality of Fender products. He was taken by the consistency of these comments, and he took that information to heart when he began working for Fender.

This lessening of quality led to a demand for higher quality instruments. One element of this was an increased interest in used instruments, and prospective customers dissatisfied with new American instruments looked to those of earlier eras. A second aspect was that new companies sprang up in America to fill the void. Mossman, Gurian, Taylor, Jackson, Kramer, Gallagher, and others were established to meet the needs of musicians who felt that they could no longer depend on Martin, Gibson, and Fender. Some of these companies met with success, but others, experiencing the same market forces as more established companies, eventually faced failure.

With the benefit of hindsight it is easy to see how poor decisions by the corporate culture led to the near demise of great American guitar companies. The intention, of course, was not to destroy companies; the intention was to make a profit. While this is certainly not anathema to the American economic system, a repetition of bad decisions made solely for short-term profit ended

Size 2

Size 2 is available in three models, each differing somewhat in materials. All three have the finest machine heads available at any price.

S2M has mahogany back and sides. It has a light, mellow sound and is the least expensive of the Gurian guitars.

S2R features East Indian rosewood back and sides. A mellow sound with the sweetness of S2M but slightly more precise.

S2R3H has a three piece back, full herringbone decoration of the bindings and machine heads that are heavily plated in real gold.

Size 3

The size 3 also comes in three models. It is a middle-size instrument with great power, brilliance and sustain and has become a standard for recording work.

S3M, an excellent instrument for solo or accompaniment, comes with chrome machine heads.

S3R has East Indian rosewood back and sides and a slightly more solid and precise sound.

S3R3H is more beautifully decorated and inlaid, with 3-piece back, herringbone binding and gold plated machine heads.

Gurian Guitars
Catalogue page

up having long-term consequences which ranged from disappointing to disastrous.

The production and sale of guitars is much the same as that of any other product. A rough guess is that about 70% of the process is quite similar to making and selling cars, toasters, cameras, or other consumer goods. Raw materials are purchased, machinery is assembled, labor is applied, and finished products result. Yet there are several elements that distinguish the process. In particular, guitars have little value if they cannot be played. Like other musical instruments, they exist to make music. There is significant evidence to suggest that success in the musical instrument industry requires a passion for the music they make. Among other problems that beset the United States' guitar industry in the 1970s through the middle of the next decade was a lack of understanding by those running guitar companies of the music made by guitars. This is part of the 30% that distinguishes the guitar industry from others. Repeated experience in manufacturing, marketing, and retail has shown that an inability to recognize that unique 30% is often the undoing of many who attempt to enter the field.

With all of the problems that were part of the American economic, political, social, and musical landscape in the years from 1975 to 1985, it was this fundamental lack of understanding and passion that drove Fender and Gibson to the brink of disaster and certainly made for lack of improvement at Martin and Guild. That fundamental understanding can't be purchased, yet without it success may be impossible.

By the 1970s American guitar manufacturers were well aware that they were selling to a global market. In 1979, 65% of Fender's gross sales were made outside of the United States. Yet, like other industries, they did not seem to understand that a fundamental shift had taken place in the economic environment. They were used to the idea of dominating a global market instead of competing in it. It was a rude awakening to find that "Made in USA", which Gibson began stamping on the back of their headstocks in 1970, was not enough to make an instrument salable. By 1985 there was a world of alternatives for the guitar buying public. American guitar manufacturers would strive throughout the next decades to reestablish their reputations, their quality, and market share.

In 1985 and 1986 the conglomerates sold off their guitar companies. Fender was sold to a group led by Bill Schulz, a music industry veteran, who had been earlier hired by CBS to turn the Fender Company around in 1985. The next year Gibson, now bordering on bankruptcy, was sold to a group led by Henry Juszkiewicz, a Harvard MBA, who had started to play guitar in high school. Also in 1986, Avnet sold the Guild Guitar Company to a group of investors.

The task of rebuilding reputation and quality was going to be an arduous one. A change in markets after 1986 significantly increased the demand for guitars. Thoughtful effort was needed to insure that American guitar companies would play a major role in this resurgence.

CHAPTER NINE

"And the first one now will later be last..."
– Bob Dylan

Starting in 1969, and running full throttle into the twenty-first century, some of America's most well-known guitar makers have borrowed from their pasts to promote and sell their instruments. Looking at their own history may seem like a normal and logical step for companies who had held and then lost unchallenged dominance in their field, but for a variety of reasons it was not. The process was neither a simple one, nor did it occur in a straightforward manner. Instead, the largest American guitar companies in the 1970s—Fender, Martin, and Gibson—all took hesitant and incremental steps towards reissuing their hallmark guitars of the past.

The decision to make reissue guitars was in some ways antithetical to American business practices, which had typically stressed innovation. The reasons for this stem back to the late nineteenth century, when the United States became the world's industrial powerhouse. Its production, in fact, exceeded that of the United Kingdom and Germany, its two closest rivals. In the late 1800s, Americans were inventing new production techniques, new distribution techniques, and entirely new products. This was the forerunner of the consumer economy we have today, where approximately 70% of the American economy is based on consumer purchases.

There were four elements that drove the full creation of the consumer economy. The first of these was the introduction of a vast array of new products during the twentieth century. The spread of electricity to homes created a demand for new devices that could be powered electrically. These included refrigerators, washing machines, radios, phonographs, and many more goods that led to a consumer boom throughout the 1920s. After World

War II this trend continued. Televisions, home air conditioning, garbage disposals, and computers are just a few of the many new consumer products that have emerged since 1945.

A second factor was the emergence of the financial services industry. This introduced the phrase "buy now pay later" during the 1920s, and evolved into the massive consumer credit industry that exists today. Prior to that era, financing was used for large purchases such as houses and farms, but had not been used for consumer products. There were some exceptions to this when it came to instrument sales. The Gibson Mandolin-Guitar Company, for instance, offered installment buying to its customers through its owner/agents, but this was on a limited basis prior to the 1920s. After that time installment buying would be used by many consumers to purchase various products, such as radios, that sold in very large numbers.

Americans also experienced an increase in household income throughout the twentieth century. According to the Bureau of Labor Statistics, the average American income in 1972 was just over $10,000, and by 2002 it had increased to approximately $50,000. Adjusted for inflation, $10,000 in 1972 had the value of $43,000 in 2002. Americans had a real gain in income. Families also spent a larger portion of their household income on non-necessities. Spending on nonessentials rose from approximately 36% in 1980 to 50% in 2002. There were more products, more money available to spend on them, and more financing options, all of which contributed to the growth of American consumer culture.

Suburbanization after World War II heralded a boom in homebuilding and buying. A wide range of consumer products are necessary to equip a new household and new households were being established very quickly. This was the period of the baby boom. Between 1946 and 1964 there was a significant increase in birth rate. This not only led to larger households, but later the creation of a youth culture that would drive much of the American economy. This new culture also impacted American music and the instruments upon which it was played.

There were two additional driving forces in the American consumer economy. One of these was the growing ability of American industry to make more products than could be justified by demand. One of the most striking examples of this was J. B. Duke, who would later found the American Tobacco Company. He was a great believer in pre-rolled cigarettes, and believed that their sleek modern look, combined with their convenience, could become a major part of the American tobacco industry. While this may seem obvious to modern readers, at the time Duke was committing himself to making cigarettes, pipes and cigars were the vastly preferred option for smokers in America.

Duke's factory in Durham, North Carolina employed people who rolled cigarettes and packaged them for distribution. It was a small market and his production system of hand rolling produced a mere two hundred cigarettes a day. In 1884 Mr. Duke bought a machine that would produce 120,000 cigarettes a day. This was the game changer. The only problem was that there was no market for 120,000 cigarettes a day. This did not deter J.B., and he lost little time setting out to create a market for his new production.

Advertising created the demand that Duke needed for success. The cigarette was touted as innovative and healthful, since it was made by clean machines without the use of human spittle, as was the case with cigars. Advertising showed people in various walks of life happily smoking away. Duke had found a way not simply to meet demand, but to create it.

There was still another way to create demand—convince people that the item they owned was outmoded or out of fashion. The perception of *new* was far more important than the reality, since it was not necessary that any change to a product be significant. The companies that produced cigarettes or gasoline had the great advantage in that their products disappeared or were disposed of after use. The makers of more durable products had to take a different approach, and the automobile industry is a prime example of this.

Henry Ford perfected his moving assembly line and his Model T, which sold over fifteen million vehicles during its lifetime. In the process he changed the automobile from a plaything for the wealthy to a ubiquitous fixture in American life. His original production techniques created a car that became increasingly less expensive (less than $300 in 1925) and brought it within financial reach of many Americans. The Model T was cheap, reliable, and steadfast.

Ford moving assembly line

Ford dominated the market with the Model T, and his success was not unnoticed by others. There were soon many automobile companies in the United States. Two, General Motors and the Chrysler Corporation, grew large enough to eventually challenge Ford. They offered cars that were competitively priced and offered new features that Ford did not—change and choice. General Motors offered a range of vehicles from the modest Chevrolet to the elite Cadillac, and both General Motors and Chrysler began a system where they would introduce new features and new designs on an almost annual basis by the late 1920s.

Automobile technology was changing rapidly and a variety of these innovations were quite valuable and convenient for the consumer. The fuel gauge, for example, became commonplace on competitors vehicles but was absent on the Ford Model T. Other additions were merely based on cosmetics. The intent of constant redesign was to convince people that their present car was outdated and that the new styling and new features warranted purchase of a newer model. Ford steadily lost market share to these ever-changing brands.

Ford tried to reclaim his hold on the industry with the Model A in 1928. The new car offered more color choices and features than the Model T, but the idea at Ford was to follow the precedent set with the Model T, and stick with the Model A design over time. The plan did not work, and after four years the Model A was retired. The American consumer obviously preferred the annual changes offered by GM and Chrysler.

In the same way that J. B. Duke had stimulated sales for his vast output of cigarettes, automobile companies advertised their new features and designs to create demand. The used car industry would not even exist if those who first purchased an automobile drove it until it had no utility. In the end, style and perception had trumped engineering and practicality.

The twentieth century had seen great changes in musical tastes and musical instruments. The steel-string, flattop guitar, the arch top guitar, the electronic pickup, the solid body guitar, and the resonator guitar all had been developed by 1960. There would be changes and modifications in the future, but the principle features of guitars had become well established. This preceded the explosion of guitar-based music that began in the 1950s and came to fruition in the mid-1960s.

Throughout the 1960s and into the '70s, guitar companies were hard-pressed to keep up with demand. Guitar making seemed to be profitable business, and companies like CBS, which purchased Fender in 1965, and Norlin, which purchased Gibson in 1969, had good reason to believe that they had made wise purchases. Along with Martin, they increased production to meet what seemed to be an ever-growing demand. That demand would, however, soon wane.

The rush to increase production, and hence profits, led to an era of poor quality that was quickly recognized by many prospective guitar buyers. After making changes to their designs, Fender had introduced new models which were not successful. Gibson also made a variety of changes to many of its instruments. The company's flat top guitars were both too heavy and badly constructed, and their solid body guitars lacked the design features and quality of an earlier era. Martin, who had opened a new factory in 1968, remained in family hands, but the quality of their products suffered.

Advertising by Gibson and Fender in the 1970s introduced changes and new models to their product line, as had become common in nearly all segments of American production and sales. The companies assumed that changes would entice new buyers and at the same time compel musicians to trade in their old for the new. Simply put, this approach did not work.

Change had come to the musical instrument market, but had been largely bypassed by Martin, Gibson, and Fender. There were, however, several successful guitar companies that emerged in the 1970s and '80s. One category of growth was the "heavy metal" guitar. Guitars made by Grover Jackson and Kramer became very popular with their locking tremolos and nuts combined with radical shapes and finishes. In 1985 Kramer, who had the exclusive rights to use the very effective Floyd Rose tremolo system, was the best selling guitar in America. These instruments were tightly bound to "heavy metal" music and their fortunes rose and fell on the popularity of this one style. While both brands are still in existence today, they take up a relatively small part of the market. Both Fender and Gibson tried to make inroads into the same market but their attempts failed.

Another area of guitar-related expansion was in signal processing. A vast array of analog, and later digital, processing equipment became available. By the mid-1980s it was common to see huge racks of gear and/or pedal boards as part of a guitar player's basic equipment.

Two American companies emerged during the 1970s and '80s that managed to combine innovation with tradition. Taylor, with its bolt-on neck attachment system, its neck profile and aesthetics, and Paul Reed Smith, with its extremely well-made, artful, and musically flexible instruments, filled the gap that had been created by the relatively poor quality of the traditional instrument makers. Both Taylor and PRS found a "sweet spot" between tradition and innovation that allowed them to become mainstays in the guitar industry by the dawn of the twenty-first century.

Grover Jackson made very well respected instruments for the metal market

Gibson, Fender, and Martin were under great economic stress by the mid-1970s. It was essential that they find some way to at least survive and, hopefully, regain their positions.

All three companies were startled to find that their used instruments were selling for more than their new ones. Not only did a 1930s D-18 sell for more than a new one made in 1975, so too did a D-18 made in 1955. A new jargon subsequently entered the guitar market. "Pre-CBS" became a common phrase referring to the Fender guitars made before CBS had purchased that company. Musicians were also actively seeking Gibsons made prior to the 1970s. By the early 1970s guitar stores featuring used instruments were becoming increasingly common, and there was a growing vintage market.

1985 Taylor

Guitar players like Eric Clapton and Mike Bloomfield, and groups like Crosby, Stills, Nash and Young, preferred older guitars. They did not do so because the instruments were collectible or fashionable; they played them because they sounded better. The older guitars were superior in many ways, but most important was that they had a sound that was not attainable with new instruments. The gap in quality between the older production and that of the 1970s was becoming obvious to professionals, amateurs, and manufacturers alike.

Asian makers had seen an opening, and began to make very authentic recreations of classic American guitars. Tom Wheeler, former editor of *Guitar Player* magazine and author of the groundbreaking book *American Guitars*, notes that the Ibanez reissue Flying V that he first saw in Los Angeles was a much more authentic re-creation than Gibson's own 1970s Flying V. Brands like Ibanez, Greco, and Tokai were crafting surprisingly accurate reissues of American guitars. American makers did not immediately pick up on the efficacy of this approach, since they remained wedded to innovation, and were still trying to make updated or improved versions of their guitars.

Mike Bloomfield, who some say started the re-popularity of the sunburst Les Paul

As American automakers were pushed to improve on the quality and design by Asian manufacturers, so too, were American guitar companies. A key difference is that carmakers continued to look exclusively ahead in their designs while guitar manufacturers came to discover that much of their future lay in the past. The idea of reissues was swimming upstream against the conventional wisdom of American industry.

This issue was apparently not discussed in those terms at any of the three major guitar companies. They were simply looking for ways that they could increase sales, and it became increasingly obvious that the new music was being dominated by new companies. Those who wanted to play traditional guitar-based music favored earlier models over the new.

The rush towards reissues followed changes in management at Martin, Fender, and Gibson. Perhaps it was easier for new management to disregard the changes that had been made by their immediate predecessors and embrace what was seen as past glories.

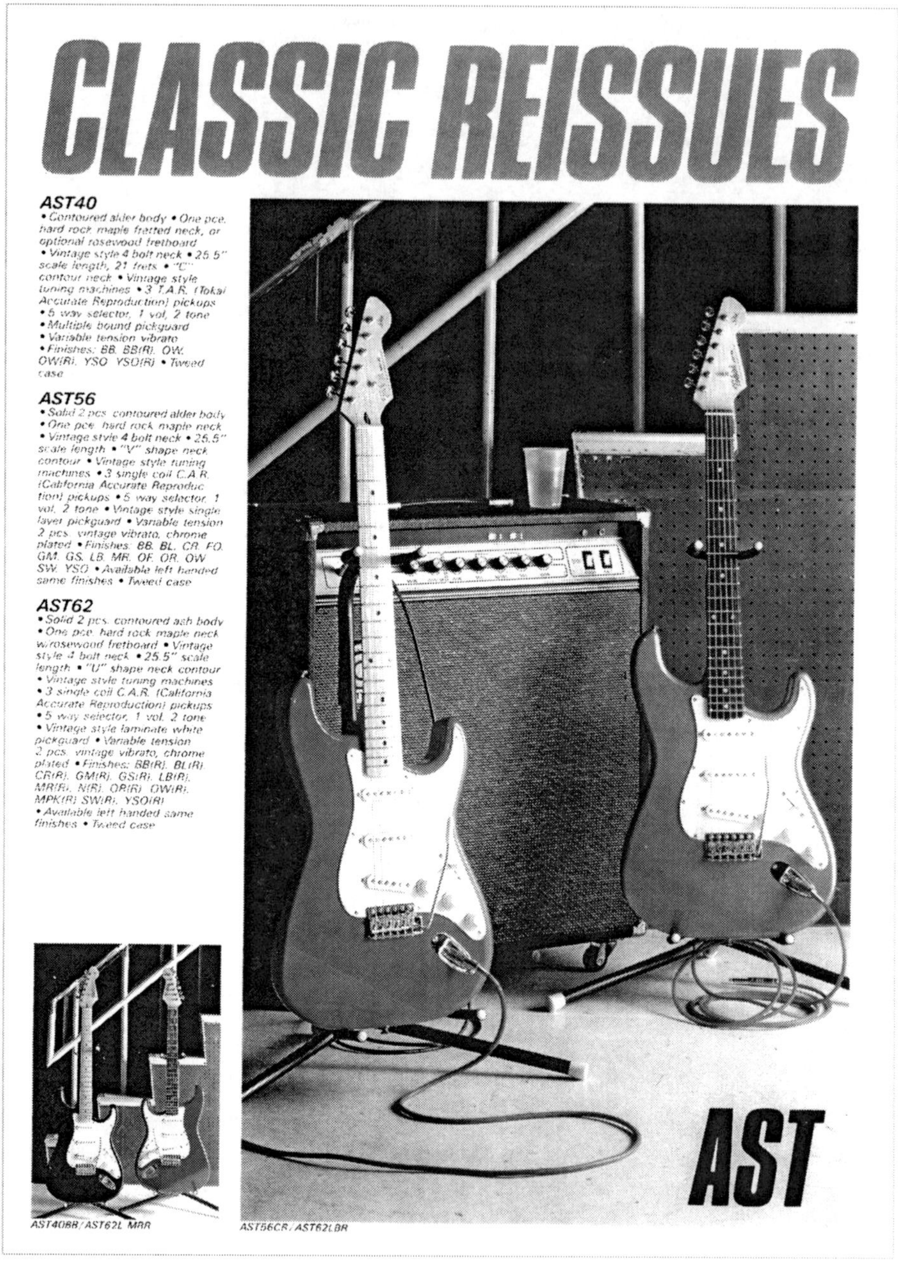

CLASSIC REISSUES

AST40

• Contoured alder body • One pce. hard rock maple fretted neck, or optional rosewood fretboard • Vintage style 4 bolt neck • 25.5" scale length, 21 frets • "C" contour neck • Vintage style tuning machines • 3 T.A.R. (Tokai Accurate Reproduction) pickups • 5 way selector, 1 vol, 2 tone • Multiple bound pickguard • Variable tension vibrato • Finishes: BB. BB(R). OW. OW(R). YSO YSO(R) • Tweed case

AST56

• Solid 2 pcs. contoured alder body • One pce. hard rock maple neck • Vintage style 4 bolt neck • 25.5" scale length • "V" shape neck contour • Vintage style tuning machines • 3 single coil C.A.R. (California Accurate Reproduction) pickups • 5 way selector, 1 vol, 2 tone • Vintage style single layer pickguard • Variable tension 2 pcs. vintage vibrato, chrome plated • Finishes: BB. BL. CR. FO. GM. GS. LB. MR. OF. OR. OW SW. YSO • Available left handed same finishes • Tweed case

AST62

• Solid 2 pcs. contoured ash body • One pce. hard rock maple neck w/rosewood fretboard • Vintage style 4 bolt neck • 25.5" scale length • "U" shape neck contour • Vintage style tuning machines • 3 single coil C.A.R. (California Accurate Reproduction) pickups • 5 way selector, 1 vol, 2 tone • Vintage style laminate white pickguard • Variable tension 2 pcs. vintage vibrato, chrome plated • Finishes: BB(R). BL(R). CR(R). GM(R). GS(R). LB(R). MR(R). N(R). OR(R). OW(R). MPK(R) SW(R). YSO(R) • Available left handed same finishes • Tweed case

AST40BB/AST62L MRR

AST56CR/AST62LBR

AST

"Classic Reissues" from the Tokai Company of Japan

It would be a mistake to think that there had been no thought given to earlier instruments prior to the wave of reissues that would begin in the 1980s. In 1968 Gibson had reintroduced the Les Paul, which was a fairly accurate reproduction. The company did not call it a reissue but rather a *reintroduction*, and quickly made modifications to it. Similarly, Martin reintroduced the D-45, also in 1968. Here, too, they did not aim to make an authentic reissue. In their advertising they emphasized the fact that it had "... details and appointments similar to the first D-45 introduced in 1937." The company also offered an HD-28 in 1976 which, while it had the scalloped bracing of the original, did not echo many of the features that would be used later with the more authentic reissues.

There is a fine line between a *reintroduction* and a *reissue*. It seems reasonable to look at the intent of the company when an instrument was produced. It was clear by the 1980s that manufacturers were not only reintroducing models similar to those of the past, but were also trying to recreate those of the past.

Fender's parent company, CBS, realized that their guitar division had become a money loser, so they brought in Bill Schulz as president, and he in turn brought in Dan Smith as director of marketing. They, along with John McLaren, the head of the musical instrument division of CBS (which included Fender guitars), had all formerly worked at Yamaha. Shultz was given a relatively free hand to make Fender profitable. There was a general recognition at Fender that the quality of their product had fallen and that Asian competitors were gaining in both market share and quality.

The company had introduced what they called a "Telecaster reissue" at the NAMM (National Association of Music Merchants) show in June, 1981. This was not an authentic reissue in any sense of the word, but rather their standard Telecaster with a black guard and a butterscotch finish. Smith, who joined Fender two months after the show, killed that project. He believed that Fender needed to make truly authentic reissues if it was to both compete with the Asian imports and reestablish its reputation for quality. To this end, reissues were designed for a '57 and '62 Strat, a '52 Tele, a '57 and '62 P-Bass, and a '62 Jazz Bass. Because of production problems at the factory these instruments did not ship until late 1982. Once they finally shipped they were very well received by the public.

The 1976 Martin HD-28 reissue

Gibson quality had fallen starting in the mid-1960s, and the decline accelerated in the next decade. During this period the company had also made significant changes to some of their most iconic instruments. For example, the company had added a volute to the back of the headstock on the Les Paul, changed from a one-piece to a three-piece neck, and constructed bodies of multiple pieces rather than one. Guitar electronics had also suffered changes in materials and quality.

In some cases Gibson management did not realize how far they had strayed. George Gruhn recalls a meeting in 1969 where it became clear that the company did not realize how much their mandolin and banjo headstocks had changed from the originals until they pulled out original templates and compared them with the modern product. In some respects, intentional changes had been made to improve production efficiency, reduce warranty repairs, or for a host of other reasons. Regardless of the cause, by the early 1970s Gibson guitars were vastly different from those of the company's glory years.

Gibson had made some attempts at reissues of solid bodies in the 1970s. Yet, with the exception of the Firebird V, the majority were not authentic reissues, but what the company considered to be improved versions. The early 1980s saw Gibson producing a variety of instruments, some of which harkened back to earlier designs. In 1980 the company issued the Heritage 80 Les Paul, and although it looked similar to the original, it was not a truly authentic reissue. In the early 1990s the company upped their game with their Historic Collection. These Les Pauls were accurate reproductions of the 1959 classic Les Pauls, down to interior routing, short stemmed pots, and other fine details. Gibson also moved the production of their custom shop/historic division to a separate building.

In the early 1990s Gibson began to make more authentic reissues of some of their iconic flattop guitars. According to Gary Burnett, who advised Gibson and provided the original Advanced Jumbo upon which the company based the reissue, the instruments from the early 1990s hold up very well against the pre-WWII guitars. Throughout the next decades Gibson would redesign an increasingly wide array of authentic flattops, including the J-45, the J-200, the Advanced Jumbo, and more, all in an effort to mirror the specifications of their golden years.

Martin guitar sales had also taken a dive. In 1982 the company sold barely over 3,000 guitars. A combination of changing musical tastes, bad management, and ill-advised modifications had put this famous American guitar company at risk. Martin switched directions in the 1970s and '80s, producing the import Sigma line and a solid body line in 1979, but none of

Reissue 1952 Goldtop Les Paul

these were highly successful. Martin's fortunes began to turn around with the ascension of Chris Martin IV into the management of the company in 1986. Dick Boak at Martin recalls that when Chris took over, the two of them were eager to try various approaches including the reintroduction of models from Martin history.

The HD-28 of 1976 had sold well, but did not herald a headlong rush into reintroductions or reissues. These were hesitant steps, as the company was trying to make its way back to profitability. Throughout the 1980s, Martin offered an evolving product mix that included new models such as cutaways and others that were actually reissues. The Custom 15 and the Custom 8 were both distinctive shop versions of the HD-28 that were significantly more authentic than the one that had been issued in 1976. The 15 and the 8 would become the HD-28V. The "V" for vintage designation came to be used more frequently and would denote this line of Martin reissues. The company now offers a variety of levels of authenticity, including the "V" series, the Golden Era series, and the custom shop Authentic Series, the latter of which replicate classic Martins in every detail.

As the twentieth century ended, reissues became increasingly common and specific. Fender and Gibson began to offer "relic" guitars. These are new instruments that are intentionally made to look as if they have years of wear. They are even offered with different levels of wear, extending from slight to heavy use. Today someone can purchase a 1952 reissue Telecaster or a 1959 Les Paul that appears to have been played for a half-century or more.

Recent Gibson Flattop reissue

The success of reissues led to an increasing market for copies of iconic vintage guitars by other makers. Players who cannot afford real vintage instruments or reissues made by the companies that had introduced them will turn to copies. Here, too, the copies can be aged to look as if they have had decades of play.

There has also been a trend to offer increasingly specific reissue instruments. These are often signature guitars which copy a particular artist's instrument down to every scrape, bump, and cigarette burn. The template may be a vintage instrument or a more recent or modified one that the notable player has previously used.

Remarkably, some instruments are being reissued today that were looked down upon when they were first produced. In particular, 1970s Fenders with the three-bolt neck and the bullet truss rod that were so quickly abandoned by the company in the 1980s are being made for a new group of consumers with nostalgia for the 1970s. It must be noted that these are well-made instruments and that their features today work far better than they did when they were first offered.

Martin, Fender, and Gibson all discovered, albeit sometimes slowly and reluctantly, that their past could be a key element in their futures. They did not, however, abandon the search for the new. All three companies have introduced new models with varying degrees of success throughout their recent histories. Some have been the artist-endorsed models, some have been innovations based on traditional designs, and some have been rather radical departures in both production and end result. Today, these companies respect their histories and pay homage to them, but there is a limit to how many guitars can be reissued. There were, after all, only so many instruments made in the past. Guitar companies continue to operate within the universe that has been a constant in the American consumer economy for more than a century. There is still an economic, and perhaps even psychological, thrust to find what will be the next innovation—the new—the next big thing.

1985 Martin D-18 V signed by C.F. Martin III and IV

CHAPTER TEN

Measuring the Immeasurable

The eighteenth century gave rise to a wave of thought that had begun with Galileo and Newton. It soon found its footing in France, and from there spread throughout the Western world. This was the Enlightenment—a movement that defined a world governed by natural laws which could be discovered and then manipulated. That idea is the basis of all modern science.

Since then a tension has existed between scientific thought, that which is measurable, and those elements of the human experience which are not. Some of these human elements are deeply held beliefs like religion, others are ideals and principles that are held by people without regard to proof, and still others are matters of taste and fashion.

The United States has been a primary battleground in this competition of ideas. Many of its Founding Fathers and its two primary political documents, the Declaration of Independence and the Constitution, were clearly influenced by the Enlightenment. On the other hand, many of the motivations that have defined American history have been driven by more abstract ideas, such as manifest destiny, justice, or equality.

This duality in the thinking processes of the Western world adds complexity to society in general and the decision-making process in particular. Are science and belief incompatible? Can these two varied approaches to human thought be complementary, rather than contradictory?

In relation to the production of musical instruments in general, and guitars in particular, this frames the debate between objective measurement/scientific

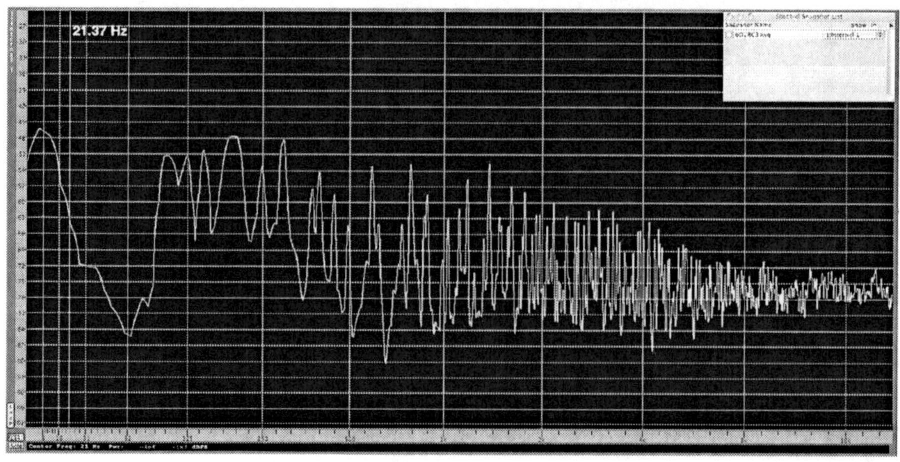

A "G" chord over time on a D-28

design on one hand and experimentation based solely on experience on the other. In the latter case objective measurement is eschewed in favor of evaluation by ear alone. There are advocates on both sides of this debate as well as in the middle. Some believe that frequencies and other elements that create the "sonic signature" of an instrument can be measured, recreated, and possibly improved as the result of this process, producing an instrument that either emulates or is superior to those of the past. Others fervently believe that no scientific testing or engineering techniques can even approximate the human ear and human experience in the creation of great instruments.

All sound is based on vibrations. In the case of acoustic guitars, as a string vibrates it then vibrates the saddle which vibrates the bridge which in turn vibrates the top of the instrument. These pulses then stimulate molecules in the air which create sound waves that our auditory system converts to nerve impulses which our brains ultimately interpret as sound. Given the complexity of this process it is a wonder that there is any agreement among any of us concerning what sounds good and why.

Although the human element involved in all of this is enormous, it is not easily measurable. One aspect is the placebo effect, which is an important part of any instrument analysis. Both anecdotal and scientific evidence makes it clear that people often hear "good" sound if that is what they expect to hear. Many instrument makers have used blind testing, where people evaluate the sound of an instrument without knowing what that instrument is, in an attempt to remove the placebo effect.

A related issue is taste. If someone believes they are hearing something that is good is it in fact *good*? Is there any objective measurement of what good sound is or can be, or is it solely defined by the listener?

Fashion also seems to play a significant role. In the 1970s it was presumed that heavier solid body guitars produced greater *sustain*, the length of time a tone is audible, and thus were desirable. This led producers like Fender and Gibson to make heavy Stratocasters, Telecasters and Les Pauls, and virtually all solid body guitar makers followed suit. By the mid-1990s, however, the idea was that the lighter the guitar the more sustain and better tone it would create. Is this simply a matter of fashion? Are "sustain" (a measurable quality), and "good tone" (which is not), being defined or even heard differently?

The role of the player is critical, as is the location where the guitar is played. These external factors cannot be controlled by the instrument maker. The goal has to be to make a great instrument. The potential players are charged with the task of selecting the instrument that will best suit their taste, desires, and needs.

There have been, and will continue to be, many attempts to define and create great sounding instruments. For about two hundred years violin makers have been trying to recreate the great instruments of the past. More recently they have devised a variety of systems to measure frequency response, volume, and other aspects that combine to make an instrument really great. Woodwind and brass instrument designers have followed suit.

In one sense those trying to recreate the sounds of outstanding instruments have an advantage. Violin builders want the sound of the Stradivarius or Guarneri, and guitar makers the sound of a pre-war D-28, a 1952 Telecaster, or other classic guitars. In these cases there is a standard which can be measured. There is a definition of "the good." They can then "reverse engineer" an instrument in every detail in an attempt to recreate its structure and, hopefully, its sound. Guitars and pickups have been taken apart and every component analyzed, including wood, wire, glue, magnets and more, to discover the secrets that lie within.

In other cases designers have tried to make an instrument with a different sound from those of the past. Their task is somewhat more difficult because they have to define "the good" without a set reference. They must determine what they think guitars of the past or present are lacking and attempt to devise methods to create those elements.

Stephen Gilchrist, one of today's most respected mandolin and arch top guitar builders, believes that there is an advantage to building an instrument for which expectations are not firmly entrenched. He says that when building his mandolins there is an expectation of sound—that of the Gibson F-5 as played by Bill Monroe—that he must meet. With his archtop guitars, which are used in a much broader context, there is no such expectation, and he has a freedom in guitar building that is lacking with mandolins.

Both of these presumptions have been, and continue to be, used in guitar production, and the techniques used have been as varied as the music that the instruments are used to play. That leads to yet another difficulty when it comes to guitars. There is not one design of a flattop guitar, for example, that is best for every type of music or every player. For instance, there is a certain sound desirable for bluegrass, but it is different from the one sought by contemporary finger style or other sorts of acoustic music. While this adds to the complexity of the process it also adds vibrancy.

There is another distinction that needs to be made. The scientific approach and the engineering approach have commonalities, but at their heart they can be quite different. Rick Turner, a well-established luthier with fifty years of experience, takes an engineering approach. He believes that his experience repairing and building guitars gives him a sense of how the instruments can be built to yield specific results. For example, should the sides of an instrument be stiffened to increase projection? If so, how should this be accomplished? He does not rely on sonic testing but instead builds an instrument with certain features to see if it meets specific goals. Success or failure is determined by the opinions of people playing and listening to the instrument.

A scientific approach to guitar design is different. Here, a range of scientific measurements are taken of an instrument. This "sonic signature" is then defined and the designers attempt to build an instrument that will duplicate this.

One of the earliest efforts in the guitar industry to create an instrument through scientific measurement was the Ovation guitar design. In 1965 Charlie Kaman, who ran a successful aeronautical company, decided to make guitars. He believed that by using techniques developed in his helicopter business he could create a guitar with great sound and mass appeal. He was not wedded to the past in terms of materials, and he thought that the back and sides of the guitar could be made of fiberglass. While his earliest experimental guitars had traditionally-shaped backs and sides, this design was soon abandoned in favor of the bowl back, which later came to be the brand's hallmark.

Martin testing

The process of designing the Ovation guitar was based on a combination of the subjective and the objective. Employees with their backs to the player would listen to a variety of guitars. Once there was general agreement about which of these guitars sounded best, their frequencies were measured with an oscillograph. Afterwards the designers would experiment with different bracing patterns and other elements in an attempt to re-create those frequencies. Thus, Ovation had a measurable goal.

The company actually built experimental guitars inside out; the bracing was on the outside of the top. In this way, subtle changes could be made to the size, shape, and placement of bracing to see what impact this would have on frequency response. Was the process successful? The late Jim Gurley, a former president of Ovation, believed that this system worked, and did yield

Ovation testing system

guitars that recreated the tones most favored in their testing. Others do not agree. For them, there is a wide gap between the sound of Ovation guitars and those of the classic guitars of the past, which were the models chosen in the testing process.

Here, the placebo effect is difficult, if not impossible, to control. When Mr. Gurley played an Ovation, he heard a guitar that had qualities similar to those of a pre-war Martin D-45. The fact that others did not experience the same is at the heart of the dilemma: How much of what is heard is subjective?

Ovation went on to be a successful company, in part because of their creation of one of the first amplification systems for flattop guitars that could be used in a live performance. There is, however, a significant group of people who believe that Ovation's innovative bowl-back design and other construction techniques produce a guitar with a superb quality of sound that is unique.

In the 1970s, Gibson, influenced by Ovation's success with their innovative approach to guitar design, created their Mark series. Here they were trying to create a guitar based on scientific principles that would be entirely exceptional. They did not test a variety of extant instruments to define their desired sound. Nor did they look back to the Gibson guitars of the pre-war era. They took an innovative approach and attempted to create an instrument with a great sound of its own that could be manufactured consistently. Several experts were consulted during the design process, most notably Dr. Michael Kasha of Florida State University. While he was not the only scientist involved in the process, his name has come to be tied to it more than any other. Richard Schneider, a well-respected luthier, was also part of the design and building process, as was Abe Wechter, who went on the create Wechter Guitars. Kasha believed that changes in bracing patterns and size, combined with a redesigned bridge and other elements, would make a great instrument.

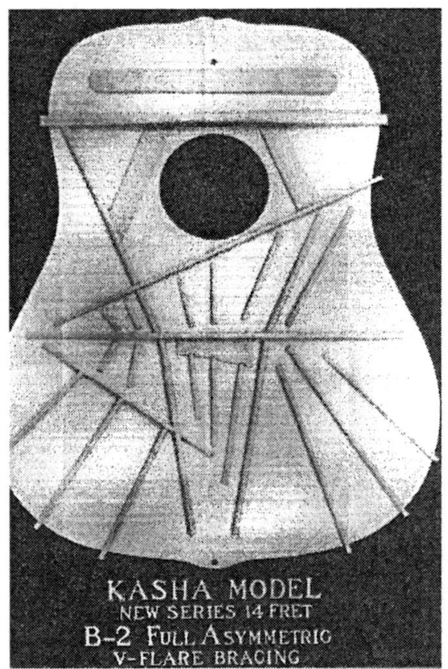

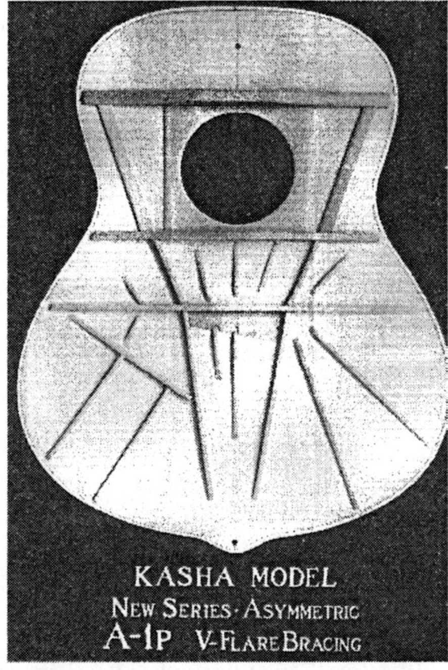

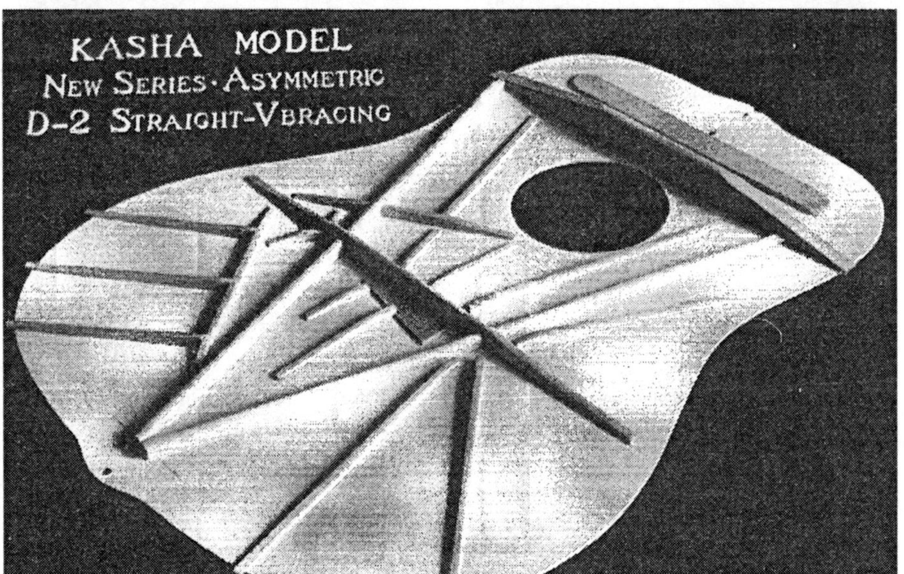

Bracing for the Gibson Kasha designed Mark series guitars

Gibson built prototypes using the principles developed by Dr. Kasha. They did not perform frequency testing to define either what they wanted or what they had achieved. Extensive testing concerning the guitar's ability to withstand changes in temperature and humidity was undertaken, and the sound of the guitar was evaluated by ear. Bruce Bolen, who was in charge of the project, believes that the Mark series was very successful in the prototype phase, but did not translate well into the production versions. He feels that shortcuts were taken in manufacturing which denigrated the sound of the guitars. Others who have played both the prototype and production models judge the former to be superior to the latter, but opine that these still were not instruments that could challenge the classic designs of the past. Again, the definition of "the good" bedevils analysis. The Mark series was not a success, and had a very short production span from 1975 to 1978.

The theory and science of instrument building has taken giant strides since the 1960s and '70s. This has originated from many areas of instrument design. Carlene Hutchens, a biologist and amateur violin maker, was a strong advocate of Chladni patterns, a technique that measures the resonant modes of tops and backs of violins. Alan Carruth, a New Hampshire luthier, has used these techniques to make guitars which he believes offer a predictable and consistent sound. Analytical techniques did not stop there; spectrographs, laser measurement, and sophisticated computer programs plot frequencies and resonance. Sometimes classic guitars are measured to discover their "magic," and in other cases prototypes are created in an attempt to make something unique and new.

Albert Germick is in charge of testing at the Martin Guitar Company, where he uses a variety of sophisticated techniques to measure both classic Martin guitars and the impact of innovation on new guitars. He believes that while testing can point in important directions, it does not hold final answers. He says the company can measure the "sound signature" of a prewar D-28, reverse engineer the instrument, and create their D-28 Authentic that reproduces that "sound signature." In the end, however, it does not sound exactly the same. While the measurable frequencies may be identical, the amplitude, here defined as volume, is not. So the overall sound, while very close, is not identical.

Matt McPherson, of McPherson Guitars, has also used a combination of objective engineering and subjective analysis in making his guitars.

McPherson, a steel and guitar player, believed that there was a better way to construct a guitar. As the owner of the largest archery company in the world, his success has been based on learning the engineering and production of bows. In particular, he stressed damping the vibration of a bow. That study in reverse became a guideline to making guitars with more vibration. Hundreds of prototypes went into making the McPherson guitar, which has been designed using a combination of science and speculation. The determination of sound quality, however, is entirely left to human beings and their definition of good sound. McPherson has listened critically to each instrument and brought in respected musicians to do the same.

Yet another important element to successful guitar building is the impact of time and vibration on the sound of instruments. Rick Turner, among many others, strongly believes that wooden instruments change in tone as they are played. In the magazine *Premier Guitar* he wrote, "I can state unequivocally that there are *huge* tonal changes in the first 24, 48, and 72 hours of stringing up a new guitar." That difference may be magnified over decades of playing.

The Tonerite Company agrees, and makes a device that simulates the effect of playing an instrument over time. Their belief is that the tone of any wooden instrument is improved with stimulation, whether that comes from being played or from their device. The inventor, Augie Lye, did extensive testing on cellos, violins, guitars, and other instruments. He found that the harmonic frequencies of an instrument in relation to the fundamental tone increased significantly with the application of the Tonerite process. The fundamental frequency is the lowest tone produced. Nodes and anti-nodes are the harmonics which add complexity to sound. It is, he says, this increase in harmonics that gives richness and complexity.

There is also a common belief that wood, even that which is thoroughly dried prior to production, and the finish applied to it after an instrument is built, both continue to dry and undergo chemical changes over time, and this impacts the tone of guitars. If this is the case, an instrument built today, no matter how good it may sound, may need decades to reach its full potential.

Others believe that building instruments using alternative materials can create great results that do not need time to reach their full potential. Some violin makers believe that the classic instruments of the past took maple and spruce as far as it can be taken. They do not believe that the exact same materials are available today, and that even if they were it would take centuries for the instruments to achieve the spectacular tone of, say, the Stradivarius. Instead they are using alternative materials in an attempt to create new instruments equal to those of the great masters.

A McPherson guitar

This approach is similar in some ways to what Ovation did in the 1960s, with the fiberglass bowl, and continues with companies such as McPherson, Composite Acoustics, Rainsong, and others. McPherson uses carbon fiber in some elements of their guitars and also uses different bracing, some of which is made by laminating spruce and rosewood. Rainsong and Composite Acoustics are making their instruments completely out of carbon fiber.

Guitars are always trying to pull themselves apart. There is approximately 183 pounds of pull on a flattop guitar strung with medium gauge strings. A guitar that is constructed with a thick top and braces to withstand the pull of the strings will hamper vibration, so the guitar will not sound good. On the other hand, a guitar can be made so lightly that it vibrates very freely, which produces great sound, but in the end it may not be strong enough to last.

Certain woods are traditionally used to make guitar tops because they have a superior stiffness-to-weight ratio. That is, they are strong while at the same time light enough to resonate. Spruce has these qualities, and has come to be the most desirable wood for acoustic guitars. But there are ongoing experiments using other woods, and fir may soon be a viable alternative.

Carbon fiber is seen as an option to wood because of its impressive stiffness-to-weight ratio. A carbon fiber guitar can be built that is lightweight and very resonant, and still be strong enough to withstand the constant pressure of the strings.

Rainsong, the earliest maker of the all-carbon fiber guitar, does not use scientific testing and measurement in their design. They build instruments as prototypes and then send them out to musicians for feedback. Then, by changing the weave and the thickness of the material, they can modify the instruments to change tone or increase volume.

One area that would seem to be ripe for testing and re-engineering is pickup design. After all, a pickup is a rather simple device made of magnets, bobbins, and magnet wire, all of which, unlike wood, are all inorganic materials. Pickup designer Lindy Frailin has been working for more than thirty years in the development of pickups. The great examples from the 1940s and '50s were hand wound so that it is impossible to define a specific standard for how tight the winding is on any specific pickup. This, along with changes in materials—including magnets, wire, and wire coating—and the impact of years of playing, make it nearly impossible to exactly recreate that which had been done.

Frailin has performed extensive testing with high-tech equipment and has used the same guitar to test his pickups for thirty years. His conclusion is simply that there are too many variables to re-create exactly what was done in the 1950s. That does not mean that manufacturers today cannot make great sounding pickups or that they cannot make pickups that sound like those of the past. They cannot, however, do frequency analysis of the pickup, or create a pickup with the same frequencies, and thus guarantee the same sound.

Tom Holmes, a Tennessee pickup maker, recalls oscilloscope testing of pickups in the 1970s. He found pickups from the 1950s had much more complex harmonics than those of the 1970s. Like Frailin, he believes that there are too many variables in materials and production methods to exactly reproduce the pickups of the past, even when their "sonic signatures" can be accurately measured.

A "CA" guitar—these, like the Rainsong, are entirely made of carbon fiber

Ned Steinberger developed new designs for solid body guitars and basses in the 1970s and '80s. He used an approach similar to Rick Turner's by stripping the guitar down to its basic components and creating his instruments by rethinking each component separately. Scientific testing and evaluation were not part of his process. While this may change in the future, he believes that art trumps science in today's instrument design.

Mark French of Purdue University literally wrote the book—actually several books—about the theory and practice of engineering guitars. He has analyzed the structure of guitars and their dynamic behavior, and has created analytical models for building them. While he believes that a great deal can be learned from testing and science, these tools can be used only to point direction; they do not tell the whole story. He has done testing for many years and is convinced that it can be remarkably helpful. In particular it can point out how changes in construction or material can impact sound. But in the end it yields an incomplete picture.

Kristin Benson, an IBMA (International Bluegrass Music Association) Bluegrass Banjo Player of the Year, recalls being in a studio trying to fix one small part of a banjo track she had recorded at another studio. The engineer pulled up her banjo track and matched the frequencies of the recorded and live sound exactly. While the frequencies looked to be identical, the sound was not, and Ms. Benson ended up re-recording the entire track.

July 28, 1959 S. E. LOVER 2,896,491

MAGNETIC PICKUP FOR STRINGED MUSICAL INSTRUMENT

Filed June 22, 1955 2 Sheets-Sheet 1

INVENTOR.

Seth E. Lover

BY

Attorney.

Seth Lover Gibson Pickup drawing

Taste, fashion, science and human perception all play an important part in making stellar instruments. Science can narrow some choices and point in different directions but its application is limited. The interpretation of the sound and feel of a great instrument by human beings is limitless. The subjective human experience with sound simply may simply be beyond that which can be quantified.

Neither Antonio Stradivari nor Christian Frederick Martin, Sr. had sophisticated equipment to test or define "the good." Perhaps there is an analogy to Supreme Court Justice Potter Stewart's famous comment about pornography. It is difficult to define, but "I know it when I see it." We may not be able to define good sound, but we know it when we hear it and the way we hear it may vary for different people and types of music. Music is central to the human experience and it is somehow comforting that the creation of great instruments encompasses a human element which in many ways confounds quantification.

The Enlightenment ushered in a new approach to how human beings interact with the material world. Everything from antibiotics to flight has come from an inherent belief that the world operates in ways that can be understood and controlled. We know that sound is produced in measurable waves. We know that certain construction techniques and materials yield predictable results. Yet, there is no objective and timeless definition of "the good." Plato tried to do it 2,500 years ago and there is today still no consensus about what he meant. To quote the immortal Sonny Bono, "the beat goes on."

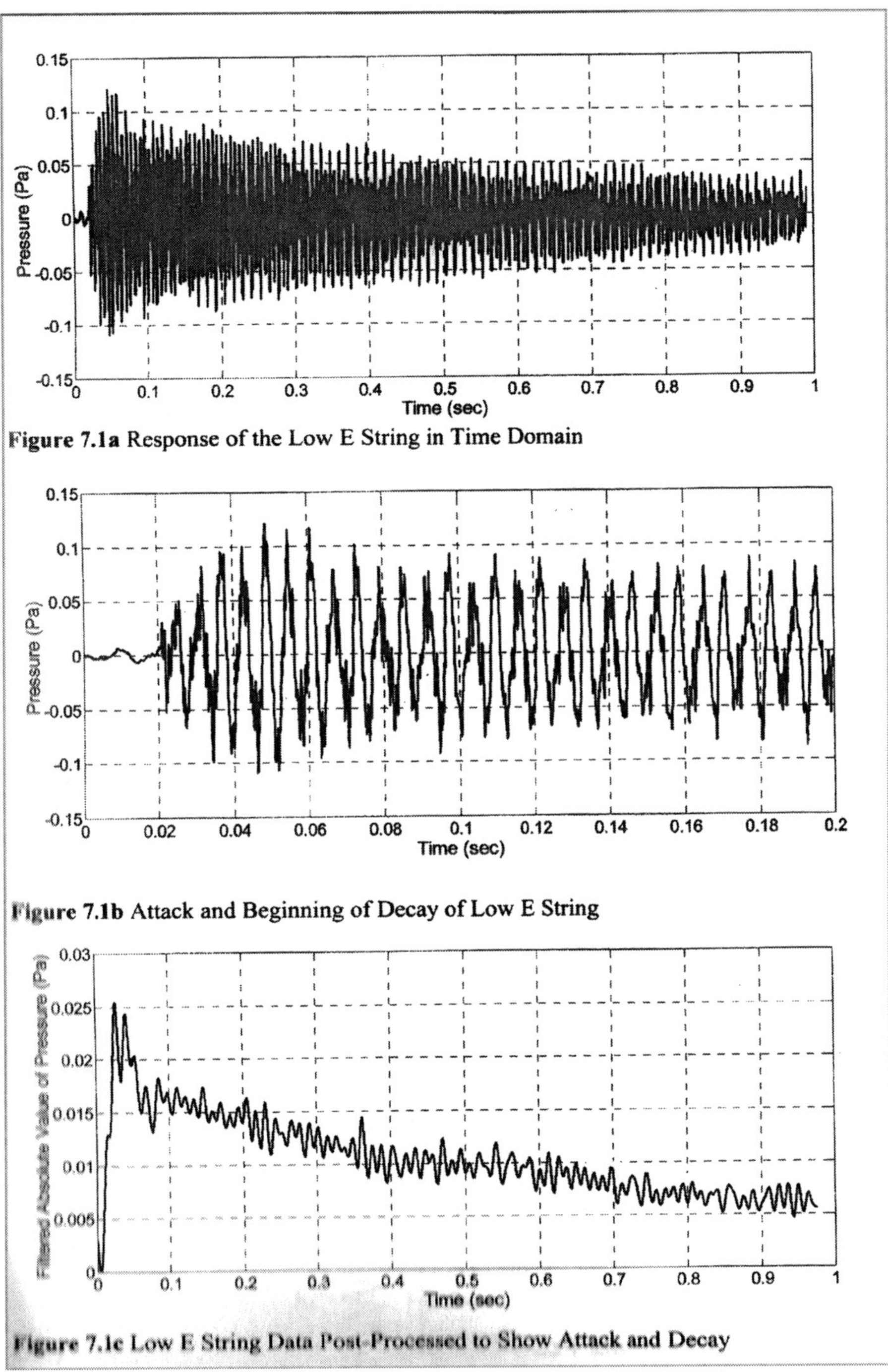

Figure 7.1a Response of the Low E String in Time Domain

Figure 7.1b Attack and Beginning of Decay of Low E String

Figure 7.1c Low E String Data Post-Processed to Show Attack and Decay

A page from Mark French's *Engineering the Guitar*

CHAPTER ELEVEN

Exuberance Irrational and Otherwise

On December 5, 1996, in the midst of the Dot Com Bubble, Alan Greenspan, then Chairman of the Federal Reserve, used the phrase "irrational exuberance." He maintained that the market value of some of the new technology stocks may have been irrationally inflated. In some quarters Greenspan was pilloried. It was said that he was trying to put a damper on a booming economy when a great deal of money was being made. Greenspan went on to explain that in the long term stock values should be tied to the profitability of companies. In the mid-1990s stocks of tech companies that had no record of profitability whatsoever were selling at very high valuations. Although a few of them ultimately became profitable, many faded into extinction. It was a classic economic "bubble."

The term "bubble" has been around for centuries. It describes a situation when prices are inflated—because demand has exceeded supply—to such a degree that price has little connection to the actual value. In the middle of a "bubble," however, what later will become conventional wisdom—that all bubbles must burst—is ignored, as profits continue to roll in.

Surprisingly, one of the most dramatic bubbles took place in the flower business. In the seventeenth century tulip bulbs in Holland were selling for outrageous prices. At its peak a single bulb, the rare *Semper Augustus*, sold for the same price as a very nice house in Holland. The "tulip bubble" was remarkably short-lived. It began in November of 1636 and had burst by February of 1637. It has become the archetype for an inflated market and is often used as a cautionary tale in business schools and economics classes. Nevertheless, it is a lesson that has often been ignored by investors in the intervening centuries.

Much of the language used during repeated periods of what later come to be recognized as grossly inflated prices has been the same over time. Prior to the crash of 1929, economists were touting the stock market as a source of ever-increasing wealth that would make everyone rich. Some said quite openly that the typical capitalist cycle of rise and fall–boom and bust—was over, and that the new wealth generator was permanent.

Much the same was said in the mid-1990s when Greenspan attracted criticism for his caution about irrational exuberance. The personal computer, the Internet, and other technological and social changes had created a world, some believed, where technology, and thus economic expansion, was unlimited. Here too, the bubble eventually burst.

Prior to the housing crash of 2007, and the subsequent economic crisis that accompanied it, financial analysts and television prognosticators said much the same thing. Real estate was a foundation investment for many Americans. One reason for this is that home owners could access their wealth by refinancing, thus freeing up money to fuel the economy. People could also get into the housing market using a variety of new financing tools that allowed just about anyone to buy a home. This was also an era when an enormous number of single-family homes—as many as 25% in 2005—were bought for investment purposes, and not as primary residences. Real estate, a traditionally long-term investment, had become a short-term one. For example, condominiums in hot real estate markets would often sell three or four times between groundbreaking and occupancy.

Mortgages were then bundled and sold to large investors. These investments were often backed up by credit default swaps, a type of insurance that in theory protected investors against default. The whole system, while profitable in the short term, was extremely precarious. The problems are obvious in hindsight, but while it was working it was working. People were making money at all levels, and supposed "experts" were saying that this great influx of wealth would continue to propel the economy indefinitely. Minor fluctuations could be expected, but those who forecast greater danger in the housing/investment "bubble"—and there were more than a few—were viewed as outliers and prophets of doom.

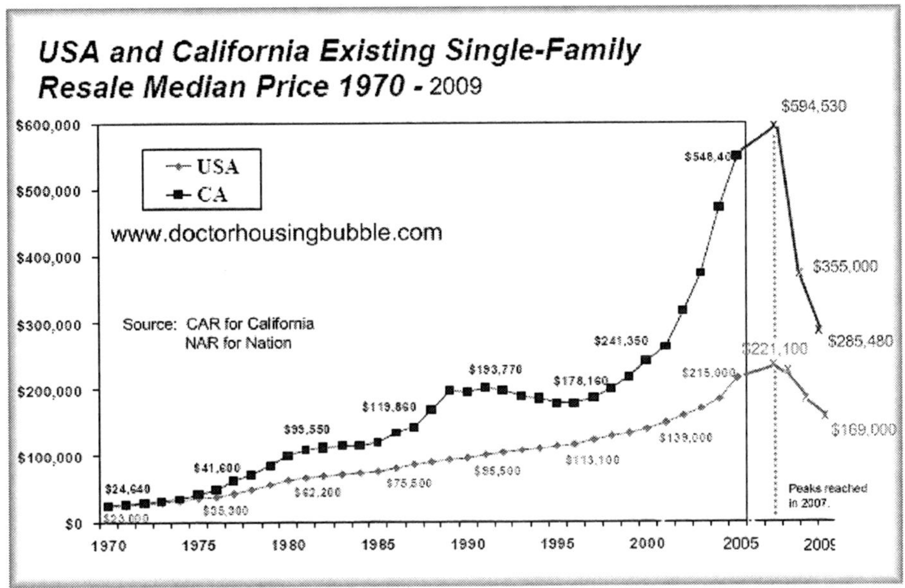

California and United States housing prices 1970-2009

Some products, such as oil, wheat, and other commodities, have a price that is often tied to utility. When people need more gasoline prices will go up, and when there is less demand the prices will go down. For tulips, art, stamps, and for our purposes guitars, the basic rules of supply and demand still apply, but utility is not a major issue. Prices for such items are determined by wants and not by needs. Certainly some instruments are desirable, some would even say essential, to play a specific type of music well, but the collector who believes he needs to have every custom-colored Strat made before 1964 is giving a very loose definition to the term "need."

In the mid-1990s some vintage guitar dealers and their customers believed that their guitar prices could never go down. This belief was based on the idea that anything that was collectible, of high quality, and with a fixed supply would continue to increase in value. To hold that opinion one had to ignore the fluctuations in the market at least since 1969. It required a particularly short memory not to recall the boom and bust of "Stratmania" that had taken hold of the market in 1987-1988 when the prices of Stratocasters rose and fell like tulip bulbs.

Tracking vintage guitar prices over time is very difficult. Guitar sale prices are not in the public record, like those of real estate, so other sources must be used to determine their worth. The *Vintage Guitar Price Guide* published by *Vintage Guitar Magazine* has tracked the value of forty-two representative vintage and collectible guitars since 1991. The *Price Guide* reflects the prices of the year prior to its cover date, so that the 2011 edition, for example, reflects prices from 2010.

The *Price Guide* index shows that the cumulative price of acquiring the forty-two representative instruments in 1991 generally rose until 1999, was somewhat flat from 1999 to 2001, climbed significantly from 2002 to 2006, then dramatically so from 2006 until peaking in 2008. In 1991 these guitars had a retail value of $153,725, in 2001 they would have cost $294,250, and in 2008, $976,200. This last year reported prices from 2007, which was the peak year for vintage guitar sales.

There are a number of factors which drove up guitar prices. First was the fact that baby boomers—those born between 1946 and 1964—had come back into the market in the mid-1980s. By this time they had disposable income and were on a quest to rediscover their youth through the music of that age. This is an interesting sociological phenomenon with musical tastes. While many things change for people as they grow older, at least in the Western world, people always seem to have a great fondness for the music of their courting years. For the baby boomers their courting years encompassed the folk boom, folk rock, the Beatles, the Rolling Stones, and Duane Eddy—in short, the era when music in the United States was dominated by guitars. By

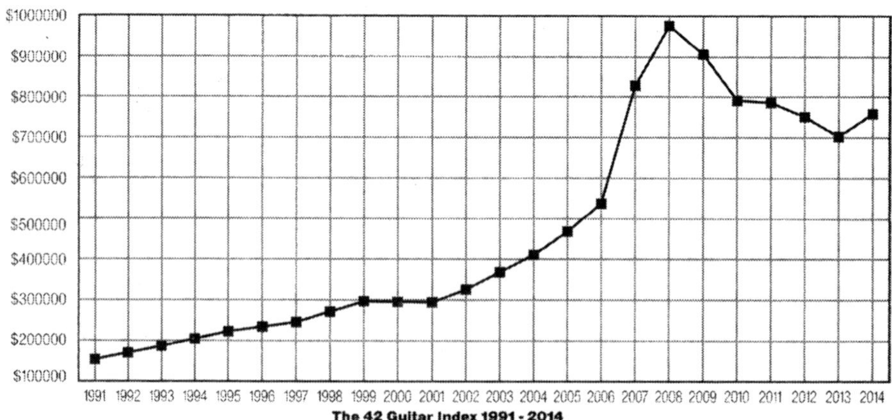

1991-2014 VG 42 Index chart

THE 42 INDEX

FROM FENDER

1952 blond Precision Bass
1952 blond Esquire
1953 blond Telecaster
1956 sunburst Stratocaster
1958 sunburst Jazzmaster
1958 blond Telecaster
1960 sunburst Stratocaster
1961 sunburst, stack knob, Jazz Bass
1962 sunburst, 3-knob, Jazz Bass
1963 sunburst Telecaster Custom
1963 sunburst Esquire Custom
1964 Lake Placid Blue Jaguar
1964 sunburst Precision Bass
1966 Candy Apple Red Stratocaster

FROM GIBSON

1952 sunburst ES-5
1952 Les Paul Model
1954 Les Paul Jr.
1958 sunburst EB-2 Bass
1958 Les Paul Custom
1958 natural ES-335
1958 Super 400CES
1959 Les Paul Jr.
1959 J-160E
1961 ES-355
1961 Les Paul SG
1964 sunburst Thunderbird II Bass
1965 EB-3 Bass
1969 sunburst Citation

FROM MARTIN

1931 OM-28
1936 00-28
1935 D-18
1944 scalloped-brace 000-28
1944 D-28
1950 D-28
1958 000-18
1959 D-18
1959 D-28E
1962 D-28
1967 GT-75
1968 000-18
1969 N-20
1969 D-45

The instruments that make up the "Vintage Guitar" 42 Index

the 1980s they were able to purchase instruments that they had lusted after as teenagers and young adults, and they began to do so.

Another significant element to the rise in guitar prices was the international market. Overseas buyers in Japan and Europe were a major force in the vintage guitar market through the 1970s and '90s. When European customers largely dropped out of the market in the mid-1980s, Japanese participation remained strong until the mid-1990s. At times, prices for vintage instruments were determined globally rather than in the United States. This was a market that was greatly impacted by exchange rates and overseas economies.

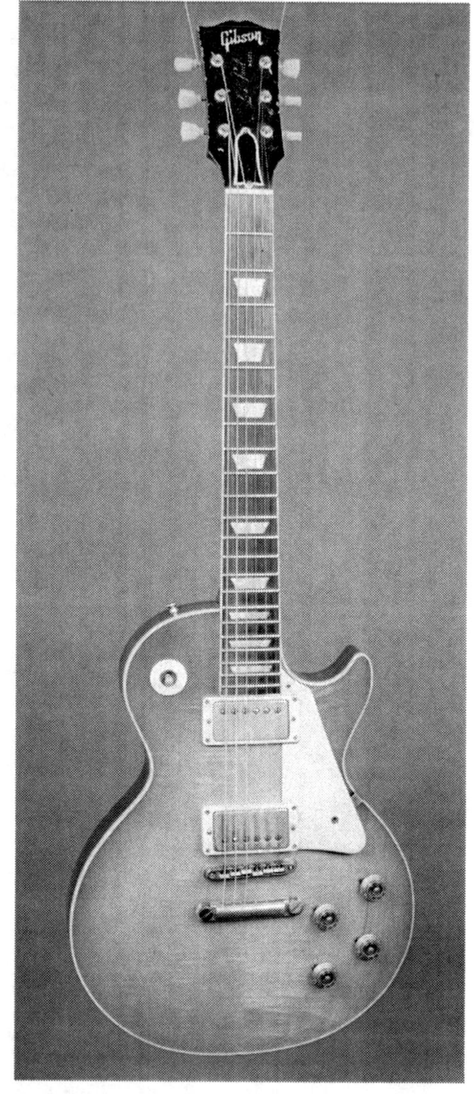

1959 Gibson Sunburst Les Paul-at the peak these sold for amounts in excess of $500,000

These buyers, both domestic and international, were passionate about guitars. Many hoped that their guitars would increase in value, but their driving force was the music, the look, or the collectability of the guitars themselves. There was a significant change in the market following 2002, coinciding with a search for high-yield investments that seemed to be endemic in American society at the time. These new buyers were primarily investors and speculators who had less interest in guitars, and more interest in making a profit from their sales.

This change may seem subtle—guitar people hoping that their guitars might appreciate, on the one hand, and investors with some interest in guitars on the other—but it is not. For the investor/speculator the fundamental use of a guitar—that is its ability to make music and all aspects that surround that function—took second place to its position as a collectible object. The differences between guitars, paintings, stamps or any other collectibles had become negligible. This significantly changed the market. People were often looking for quick returns. Instruments would sometimes change hands several times during one year, and the price would increase with each sale.

1940 Martin D-45, perhaps the most sought after flat top guitar at the peak these sold at $375,000

Some vintage guitar dealers went so far as to specialize in "investment grade instruments." They were no longer dealing in guitars. Their focus was the investment value, and they were selling investments, i.e. guitars, about which they were knowledgeable, much in the same way that real estate brokers would sell condominiums or stockbrokers would sell stocks. Like housing and other investments, this steep rise worked as long as there were buyers willing to pay ever-increasing prices.

Then came the fall. According to the *Vintage Guitar Price Guide,* the forty-two guitars that had held a retail value of $976,200 in 2008 were worth $702,625 in 2013, a drop of nearly forty percent. Guitars, like every other item in the marketplace, are worth whatever someone is willing to pay for them. If there are buyers for a 1959 Les Paul at $500,000, it is worth $500,000. If there are no buyers at that price, its value must be adjusted.

For many owners of vintage instruments the price fluctuation was merely a matter of a perception of wealth. For someone who neither bought nor sold instruments during the period from 2000 to 2013 the impact was only on paper. Dealers, collectors, and other active buyers of vintage guitars, however, suffered real and significant losses. The trick to investing during a bubble is realizing that you are in one.

The vintage guitar market was not unique. After 2007, some fine art prices also fell precipitously, as did those of other collectibles. These markets are mere specks on the economic horizon compared to the consequent disaster that befell the housing market. Between 2007 and 2012 American home values fell by approximately 33%. In some very hot markets such as California, Florida, and Nevada drops approached or even exceeded 50%. Even though the difference in scale is vast, the vintage guitar and collectible markets remain subject to some of the same forces that drive prices in the larger economy. Blind to the perils of boom and bust, people had been looking for lucrative investments and had cast a wide net in their search.

Not all of these changes in the vintage guitar market have been deleterious. While prices may have fallen, some believe that speculators had so disrupted the market that their withdrawal from it has served to make it more stable. During the run up, it was difficult to determine what the value of a particular instrument may be, since valuations were simply changing too fast. All parties—dealers, private sellers, and buyers—were impacted by this volatility.

Economics is not the only factor that has impacted the vintage market. Demographics play an important role as well. The baby boomers who had entered the market in the 1980s, and who had largely been responsible for the steady increase in vintage guitar prices, have now reached an age when they are downsizing and reducing their guitar ownership. In 2014 there are very few in that generation who are still building collections or acquiring that treasured guitar that they wanted long ago. Many have moved on to other pursuits such as cars and travel, and others have scaled back their lifestyles.

Here too guitars are not alone. The market in antique furniture and clocks, for example, has, in the opinion of Helaine Fendelman, a well-respected New York appraiser of art and antiques, "tanked." That is not to say that there are no collectors of anything. They exist and they are active; the objects of their affections, however, have changed. Instead of collecting antique furniture, a new generation is actively seeking out furniture from the 1950s and 1960s. Nostalgia seems to be a driving force. The children of the baby boomers who are now actively entering a variety of collectible markets are interested in different things than their parents. The one thing that they do not have a vast interest in is vintage guitars.

The children of baby boomers are clearly a very different market with a wide range of interests in diverse areas. Even when it comes to cars, which had been, and continue to be, central to the life of boomers, their children are less interested. Seventy-nine percent of people between twenty and twenty-four had a driver's license in 2011, while 92% of that same age group had one in 1983. In that same year, 1983, 84% of people sixty to sixty-four had a license; this increased to 93% in 2011. This is a dramatic shift in priorities from one generation to another. Demographic shifts are at the heart of some fundamental changes in the American economy and the vintage guitar market appears to be particularly sensitive to these.

This same guitar market seems to be going against one of the major economic trends of the last half-century. In many ways national boundaries have become nearly meaningless in commerce. A variety of factors help to account for the fact that items made anywhere are now available for sale everywhere. But vintage instruments, in particular guitars, seem to be going against this tide of increased international sales. There are several factors affecting this trend.

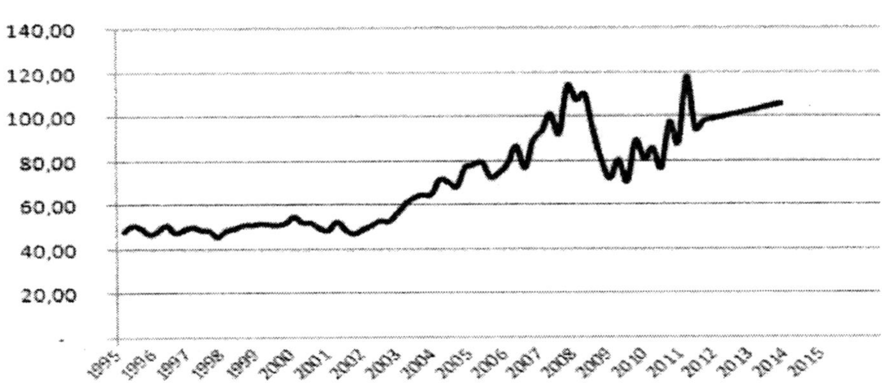

Art price changes 1995-2014

New environmental regulations make it difficult, and in some cases nearly impossible, to ship instruments containing Brazilian rosewood or ivory, a component of many vintage instruments, across international boundaries. To date these regulations are unevenly applied. Some sellers have ignored these laws and regulations, while others have almost abandoned the practice of shipping vintage instruments across national borders.

Yet another factor impacting international trade in vintage instruments is that some of the traditional markets, in particular Japan and parts of Europe, have been buying American instruments for many years. They may have reached a point of saturation, where their internal supply will feed their own national markets. The international market, one of the driving elements of vintage sales of the past, may experience a significant reduction in the future.

The vintage guitar market is changing, as it always has. There is no way to predict its future direction with any certainty. The great American acoustic guitars of the pre-World War II era or electrics from the 1950s and '60s will not lose their cachet or their utility, but in time they may lose value. The supply will not change, since producers cannot make more original 1938 Martin D-28s, 1952 Fender Telecasters, or 1959 Gibson Les Pauls. However, the demand will slow if there are fewer or less ardent buyers for these classic instruments.

Musical tastes, demographics, economics, the complexities of international trade, and the fact that very high quality new instruments are currently being made, combine to make for significant challenges in the vintage guitar market. The market can, however, turn on a dime. A significant renewed interest in the music of the 1950s and '60s, the rise of a style of music as yet unknown that comes to treasure vintage instruments, or some entirely unexpected phenomenon could lead to a resurgence in the market.

CHAPTER TWELVE

The Only Thing Constant is Change

By 1900 a wave of technological innovation, an increasingly cheap immigrant labor force, plentiful raw materials, and less expensive domestic and international transportation costs combined to make industry in the United States a threat to traditional European industrial powerhouses. The Europeans reacted strongly, complaining of unfair advantages held by their American competitors, much as American industry has complained about the influx of imported goods to the United States since the 1960s.

The modern world continues to become smaller. The transportation revolution that began with the steam engine, canals, and railroads persisted through the first half of the twentieth century and accelerated during the second half of the century. The introduction of containerized shipping in the mid 1950s played a major role in reducing shipping costs. It even became profitable to send inexpensive goods across the ocean.

Air cargo prices have also declined significantly since the 1950s with the introduction of both the jet engine and larger capacity aircraft. The expansion of the interstate highway system in the same period, and, consequently, trucking, has reduced the cost of transportation on land. These are just a few of the elements that have opened the United States market to Mexican- and Canadian-made products.

From 1950 to 2004 the value of world trade grew at an average rate of 5.9% per year. Looking only at manufactured goods, that figure is 7.2%. This is an enormous increase; production and consumption have both become global.

Virtually every American industry, including the guitar business, has been significantly impacted by international competition, especially from Asian

US-UK relative Iron prices 1880-1913

producers. This began in the 1960s and has become an increasing part of the American musical instrument market. American manufacturers looked at the invasion of these products with skepticism and concern, and not without good cause. Kay and Harmony, two large manufacturers of introductory to intermediate guitars, succumbed quickly to foreign competition. That competition has only increased. In the first six months of 2012, there were 1,378,172 guitars imported into the United States.

Guitar production has switched from country to country in pursuit of ever-cheaper manufacturing costs. Once based in Japan, low-end guitar production first moved to Korea, and has now shifted to Indonesia, China, and Vietnam.

According to *Music Trades Magazine*, Japan ranked first with 34.32% of global sales, the United States was second with 31.17%, and Germany third with 7.75%. China, with its 6.07%, lagged in fourth place. Clearly Japan and the United States are the dominant producers.

The demand for musical products, in general, reflects a similar ranking, but the spread between the United States, first, with 40.6% of the global market, and Japan, in second place with 13.1%, is quite remarkable. China comes in third with 7.1%, and Germany fourth with 6%. Japan, then, produces slightly

Modern Container Ship—each "box" carries thousands of products

more musical and audio products than the United States, while it consumes much less. Both sets of statistics underscore the fact that making and using musical instruments and audio products is not restricted by location.

The United States still remains a very significant producer of guitars and other musical instruments. The industry has not followed trends in other consumer products such as televisions, where there are no American manufacturers, or clothing, where 97% of garments sold in the United States are made outside its borders.

Nevertheless, the United States guitar industry is clearly part of a global industry, and not its sole or dominant force. There is still a cachet to American-made guitars, and most medium to high priced guitars are still made in America. That said, this situation may be about to change. For many musicians who first started to play in the 1980s, the Ibanez, Yamaha, or Alvarez brands are as familiar to them as Fender or Gibson, and several imported brands are selling at the middle or even high-end price point.

Domestic American guitar making has grown exponentially since the mid-1980s. Several guitar companies that were either nonexistent or very small

Ibanez ad reintroducing a guitar from the company's past

in 1985 are now major manufacturers. Taylor, Paul Reed Smith, G&L, Larrivee, and others now play a significant role in American production. Their output, along with that of older companies like Martin, Fender, Gibson, and Guild, yields what is likely ten times more American guitars than were made forty years ago. Martin, the easiest company to track, made

7,275 instruments in 1985 and 100,976 in 2012. Fender and Gibson apparently had similar increases. Paul Reed Smith, founded in 1985, now makes 1,000 instruments per month at its Maryland factory. Taylor created just 614 guitars in 1985 and in 2013 that number was approximately 40,000. All of the American companies also have factories in other countries making guitars for the American and global markets. In sum, there are an ever-increasing number of guitars made in the United States and overseas coming into the American market.

Schmidt and Maul from 1856 that still plays beautifully

Guitars, when well cared for, can last for many years. For many manufacturers their greatest competition is not from other companies but rather from guitars from their own past. The vast majority of guitars ever made have been produced since 1985. These are still relatively young and comprise a large part of an ever-growing market in used instruments.

Increased guitar production, both in the United States and overseas, combined with an ever increasing stock of used instruments, present an enormous challenge to the guitar industry. More instruments are going to require more players, if the guitar industry is to remain viable..

The globalization of the industrial economy that began in the late nineteenth century continues unabated. As American buyers look to overseas manufacturers, American manufacturers also look to international markets for a significant percentage of their sales and profits. In some cases this is 50% or more. The international trade in guitars is very much a two-way street.

Ease of communication is another important element to the ever-widening marketplace. The Pony Express lasted less than two years, and the telegraph soon replaced it. Although expensive to operate, since it required skilled operators, relay stations, and wires, it was revolutionary in its day. Communication time was cut from days or weeks to mere hours, as messages were swiftly relayed across the continent. The invention of the telephone increased the ease of communication, and the advent of the facsimile (fax) machine in the 1980s was a step closer to instantaneous communication of documents and photographs. The Internet, however, has left all of these older technologies far behind.

Since the introduction of the Internet it is now possible to send instantaneous communication including text, photographs, documents, voice, and video to virtually any place in the world. Manufacturers in California, Beijing, and Stuttgart all have equal access to the same worldwide market at very low cost. With new products, the lower costs of transportation, combined with faster and virtually free communication, have made much of the world one large nearly unfettered marketplace. The vintage market, however, is headed in a different direction. Small producers and retailers are also active players in the global marketplace. Ease of communication and transportation has created a system where anyone with something to sell has access to an international pool of buyers and the means to deliver it anywhere.

The same factors may eventually lead to broad changes in the distribution system for musical instruments and accessories. There has already been a steady decline in the role of wholesale companies. These businesses provided what was once a necessary intermediate step between the manufacturer and retailer. While some of these companies still exist, their importance has been undermined by the ability of retailers to connect directly with manufacturers. The growth of UPS and FedEx also makes it easy and cost-effective for a factory to ship its products in relatively small numbers. For example, dozens of sets of guitar strings can be shipped, instead of several gross at a time, to a retailer.

Not only has the relationship between the manufacturer and retailer changed, so too has the relationship between a retailer and the end-user. Large catalog companies like American Musical Supply, Sweetwater, or Musicians Friend, and a host of other companies large and small, sell their products nationally and internationally. With the exception of shipping cost, which may be free, the customer's location is virtually irrelevant.

Manufacturers continue to readjust to ever-changing circumstances. In the first days of the Internet all major manufacturers struggled to devise strategies to use the Internet effectively and, at the same time, preserve their local dealer networks. There is still a broad array of manufacturers' policies describing what can be advertised, how it can be advertised, and at what price. The protected dealer territory is now on its way to extinction, in fact, if not in theory.

The big box store model that grew rapidly in the 1990s began to separate from the traditional instruction, service, and delivery retail paradigm. These large stores, such as the giant Guitar Center and its smaller competitor Sam Ash, had good prices and selection but, until recently, did not offer instruction. The growth in the number of people playing guitars was such that these large stores could leave instruction to private instructors or independent retailers. The big stores could then sell to this pre-developed market based on selection and price.

Carvin, the California guitar manufacturing company, has been selling directly to customers for many years, and others may soon follow suit. Fender has begun to sell bodies, necks, and accessories directly to the consumer, instead of through their dealer network. Manufacturers of the future may partially or completely adopt the Carvin direct sales model.

Changes in distribution may originate from a company such as Amazon, which sells a vast array of products, with same-day delivery in some markets. The company's web of regional warehouses is increasing its ability to process and deliver orders quickly. Amazon's penetration of the guitar business is minimal as of January, 2014, and there are some aspects of guitar sales that may make it difficult to sell them like a book or paper towel holder. Nonetheless, if Amazon can gain a 5% or 10% market share, their presence would be significant.

Carvin direct order catalogue

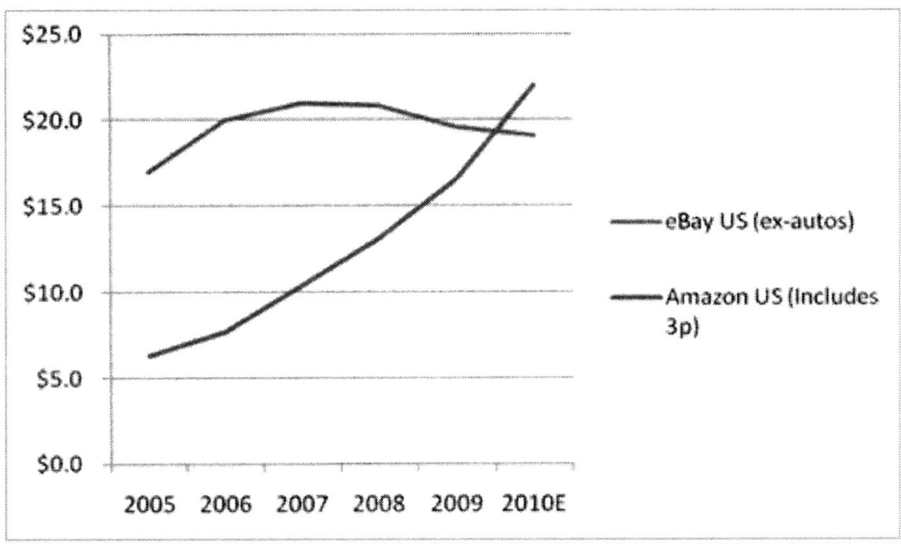

Amazon sales (including third party), the bottom line in 2005, have eclipsed eBay

Another equally important issue is the "race to the bottom." This generally refers to a public that is driven by price—the lowest price. A giant discounter like Walmart, when combined with the auction mentality of eBay and the myriad of online dealers who offer equally low prices, have encouraged consumers to expect the lowest price possible. This has impacted the guitar industry in several ways. On the positive side, it has created many inexpensive, and sometimes quite good, products, but it has also continued to narrow the margins for retailers. The simple fact is that traditional retailers in the music industry need to have a spread between what they pay for a product and the price for which they can sell it. Without this spread no business can survive, especially the traditional "brick and mortar" store, where the overhead is much higher than the online retailers. A healthy spread must cover these additional costs.

Guitar buyers may be split into two broad categories. The first are those individuals who are buying a medium price guitar made by a well-known and respected manufacturer. They know what they want and will be happy to order it from a website and get a low price with next day delivery. The other group would be people who want extra advice or a more intimate buying experience. This would include beginners who do not know what they want or need, and, at the other end of the spectrum, experienced players who want to hold a guitar in their hands before they purchase it.

While there are certainly differences between selling books and guitars, bookstores have experienced a trend in this direction. The big box book stores have suffered with their sales being taken over by Amazon. At the same time there has been some growth in small personal bookstores, for the customer who wants a more hands-on buying experience.

The key for the brick-and-mortar store may lie in the concept of *added value*. If buying a guitar is only a matter of price and convenience, Internet giants could control a significant part of the market, but the desire for instruction, service, and support, i.e. added value, could check the role of Internet giants.

Market segmentation—the division of the market into ever smaller parts—has become standard in American marketing in general, and in some respects guitars in particular. After World War II there was a relatively brief period where the American consuming public was viewed as one entity. It was said that the rich man and the poor man would use the same toothpaste, and essentially drive the same car. By the late 1950s the idea of market segmentation had become entrenched. The belief was that more profit could be gained by creating specific products or versions of products geared to well-defined market segments. Psychologists, sociologists, and advertising experts conducted broad studies that identified unique demographic groups, the products that would appeal to each of them, and the best way to motivate purchases. While not entirely new, this approach accelerated in the postwar environment.

Magazines targeted specific groups—suburban housewives, factory workers, young adults, and many more—and sold advertising aimed at each of them. This became more focused with the advent of television. Daytime shows would display different advertising than prime time shows, and programs geared for children had very different ads than those for their parents. Radio, newspapers, and virtually every other advertising-supported medium soon followed suit.

By the end of the first decade of the twenty-first century, cable and satellite television had yielded a vast array of channels geared to ever narrower audiences. Advertising on the Golf Channel is very different than that seen on MTV. The Internet has once again raised the ante. Companies are tracking every Internet search and purchase to determine which product should be pitched to ever-narrowing segments of the population. In some

World Music in Nashville offers a full lesson program and a wide variety of services to engage customers

cases, advertising is geared to a specific individual. We can expect this to continue into the foreseeable future.

The guitar industry certainly divides its market by price. There are instruments specifically designed for and marketed to players with varying amounts of money to spend. Yet in another sense there is certain uniformity to the market which goes against the market segmentation trend. Music seems to be a unifying factor. The same guitar magazine will have advertisements for very expensive and more modest instruments, even though the magazine itself is geared to one musical audience. Even a publication like *Guitar Aficionado,* which is aimed at the very high end guitar buyer, continues to include advertisements for Epiphone and other makers whose instruments are geared to a more modest buyer.

A related issue, income inequality—the concentration of wealth at the top tier of society—has political and moral implications that are open to debate, but its economic implications remain clear. The consumer accounts for approximately 70% of the United States economy, an economy which depends on a large middle class to buy a vast number of products. If that middle group shrinks as the ranks of the very wealthy and very poor grow, it will wreak havoc on the whole system. In 2014 there are a number of indicators that show this happening in several industries. In clothing, for example, the low and high ends are showing growth, while the middle is either stagnating or shrinking.

The guitar industry is not ignoring the middle, but the price extremes are getting plenty of attention. According to *Music Trades*, in 2012 there were 50,004 acoustic guitars sold between $501 and $1500, and 20,001 instruments sold for over $1501. At the lower end of the spectrum 900,066 acoustic guitars were sold with a retail value of $350 or less. Obviously there is a large market for low-end instruments. It is also reasonable to suggest that some of the models at the very low end are not actually musical instruments, but toys. There is, however, a relatively strong contingent of mid-level buyers. Many manufacturers are aiming their products squarely at the $800-$2,000 price point. This may or may not be a profitable strategy, but many producers believe that there is a strong market share to be had between the introductory and professional grade instruments.

This is all taking place during a period where young people, the traditional pool for new guitar players, have an ever-increasing array of options for their money, time, and musical creativity. There are many ways to make music in the twenty-first century that did not exist even twenty years earlier. The turntable is no longer just a device on which to play records. Instead, it has become a valid and important instrument in its own right that provides musical and creative satisfaction. There is also a great deal of computer software available for music creation. Some of the programs are complex and require a large amount of skill to master. Others are more basic, and may make the old claim of "make music today" a reality. Joe Lamond, the president of NAMM, a major music industry trade organization, editorialized that these new technologies, which simplify music-making, offer new possibilities for the music industry.

Guitars may or may not continue to be central to American music. The instrument has had quite a long run of popularity when compared with the tenor banjo, the mandolin orchestra, the home organ, or the accordion. The fortunes of any instrument are tied directly to the desire of people to play the music that the instrument produces. Music is at the core of the guitar industry. The locales of manufacture, the materials used in production, and a host of other factors may change, but the fundamental issue has been, and continues to be, whether people will continue to embrace the music made on guitars.

Some new ways to make music

Predicting future trends is hazardous at best. The period from 1976 through 1984 saw a significant decline in guitar sales, and during that time CBS and Norlin both sold their guitar companies. Some believed then that the guitar industry would never be as popular as it had been. Those predictions were, of course, entirely wrong. Guitar-based music flourished, as did the guitar industry both in the United States and in the global market.

The philosopher Heraclitus said that, "The only thing that is constant is change." In an era when ebb and flow, high and low tides, and every other analogy for change have become ubiquitous, his maxim seems to hold an essential truth. He also believed that fire was the basic material of the world. On the first point he would seem to be correct, but modern science would have some serious argument with the latter. Basic truths are, at best, illusive.

Photo Credits

Many of the photographs and other illustrations used in this book are from the author's personal collection. Some photographs of guitars came from the files of Gruhn Guitars, who kindly opened them to us.

The Fender Telecaster by Andre Duchossoir, published by Hal Leonard: photo of Leo Fender.

The History of the Ovation Guitar by Walter Carter, published by Hal Leonard: photos of Josh White and one of testing an early Ovation.

The Guitar Pickup Handbook by Dave Hunter, published by Hal Leonard: two images pickup patents drawings.

Gibson Fabulous Flattops by Whitford et al., published by Backbeat Books: diagram of Kasha bracing, Mark series photos, and photo of Robert Johnson.

Gibson Electrics by Andre Duchossoir, published by Mediapress: photos of Charlie Christian; Chuck Berry.

C.F. Martin and his Guitars by Phillip Gura, published by the University of North Carolina Press: photo of C.F. Martin.

The Encyclopedia of Country Music published by Oxford University Press: provided photographs of the Carter Family, Fiddling John Carson, and Elvis Presley.

Doug Green graciously allowed the use of a photograph of Ray Whitely from his private collection.

Some photographs and illustrations were downloaded from the Internet and it was impossible to determine any copyright or ownership.

Photo Credits

Please note: *Several attempts were made to contact publishers who either could not be found or did not reply. There has been no intent to use any photographs, illustrations, or other materials without proper permissions. Please contact us with any errors made in this regard so that they can be corrected in future editions.*

SOURCES

There is a Great Deal More to Read

This is a book of synthesis. In it, I wanted to marry some important elements of guitars, the guitar business, and guitar construction with broad themes of American history. There is a great deal of controversy surrounding many elements of the American past, but most of the issues addressed in this book are more matters of fact, at least in the broad sweep of American history. Obviously, there are interpretive elements. This book is not a list of facts but is, instead, interpretive and, even in its last chapters, speculative. This brief essay should point the reader to a variety of sources where they may find additional information.

There are multitudinous books that detail various aspects of American history, such as the War with Mexico, which led to the incorporation of California into the United States, the expansion of transportation, the era of the Roaring Twenties, and virtually all of the historic periods and themes that I've discussed. There are some fine bibliographies that can be easily accessed online addressing American social, political, and economic history. The best are those attached to a syllabus from a good college course.

One book on a specific area of American history I will mention is *A Consumer's Republic* (Vintage Books), by Lisbeth Cohen. It is a provocative and fascinating study of American consumerism after the Second World War.

The Bureau of Labor Statistics is also a very valuable source for information about household wealth, buying habits, and a variety of other useful topics. Since their data is retrospective, it is easier to observe trends. *Music Trades* magazine is also a wealth of information. This magazine, which has been in existence for many years, has closely tracked the music industry. Its information on the entire industry, and specifically on guitars, is illuminating and important.

Many people believe that online sources are invariably correct, and this is often a big mistake. While the Internet has made information widely available, its sources are often not vetted as they were in the old days when a publisher's imprint meant that there had been some peer review of the book's contents. There are some fine sources on the Internet, but there are others that should be used with caution. In other words it is best to verify and cite sources properly. The simplest and most effective way to verify a website is to check to see who sponsors it. For example, is the site affiliated with a well-respected journal or institution? When anyone can say or write anything it is wise to exercise care. Wikipedia, in particular, has some very useful information, but it is an open system that allows collaborative editing of its content, and as such should be used with due caution. In this book I have not used it as the only source for information.

I found a great deal of material concerning general economic trends and specific topics, such as violin prices, the impact of online sales for Lego collectors, the rise of eBay, income inequality, antique prices, and much more from verifiable websites. The web also proved to be an important source about the specifics of instrument design. There is a wealth of knowledge on the theory and practice of violin design that is relevant to the application of science to guitars.

With that said, the possibilities of finding original advertisements, sound and video recordings, eyewitness accounts, and a host of other materials on the Internet are incredibly exciting. Being able to dig out primary materials that have been digitized and made available to all of us has been a great pleasure, and has been remarkably informative.

Joel Whitburn's *Pop Memories:1890-1954* and *Pop Annual:1955-1999* (Records Research Press) are rich resources to find out which music was popular in different eras. The author has compiled the charts from *Billboard Magazine* and its predecessors that show record sales in detail for each year.

Some of the best books dealing with country music are the *Encyclopedia of Country Music*, (Oxford University Press), and *Country Music USA* (University of Texas Press) by Bill C. Malone, which is a richly detailed textbook on country music. It is probably the best overall examination of the genre.

There are several very good books about the blues. Paul Oliver's *The Story of the Blues* (Northeastern University Press) and several books by author and performer Elijah Wald stand out. Wald's *Short History of the Blues* (Oxford University Press) is a brief but thorough and well-written introduction to the subject.

There are fascinating books that cover the folk revival. Among them is Ronald D. Collins's *Rainbow Quest* (University of Massachusetts Press) and Robert Cantwell's *When We Were Good* (Harvard University Press). Both of these look at the social, political, and musical themes of the folk music revival that peaked in the 1950s and '60s.

Another wonderful source for studying which instruments were popular during various eras are the reprints of the Sears Roebuck and Montgomery Ward catalogs. They show which products appealed to the mass market, since these companies served a broad swath of the American public. Their catalogues are a great source for anyone wanting to look at American consumerism.

The catalogues and other sales materials from Gibson, Martin, Fender, National, Oahu, and other manufacturers and distributors illustrate what they were making and selling, and which features they thought were most significant to the consumer. In some cases these also show who the manufacturers considered to be their target markets. Some of these are available as reprints and others can be found online. They make for enjoyable reading.

There are a significant number of books that cover guitars and their history which provide the detail that this book does not. Some of these books are personal reminiscences, some take a broad view of either a manufacturer or a type of instrument, and others look very closely at details surrounding one manufacturer or instrument.

The history of Martin guitars is one of the best covered. Philip Gura's *C.F. Martin and His Guitars: 1796-1873* (University of North Carolina Press) is a comprehensive look at the very earliest instruments from this remarkable American guitar company. *Inventing the American Guitar* by Hal Leonard, (edited by Robert Shaw and Peter Sezgo) focuses entirely on Martin guitars prior to the Civil War. Richard Johnston and Dick Boak's *Martin Guitar: A History* and its companion *Martin Guitars Technical Reference*, by Hal Leonard, combine to make a very detailed and authoritative history of the company and its instruments. Walter Carter, who writes some of the most readable and well-researched of any guitar books, wrote *The Martin Guitar Book* (Backbeat Books), which is a very well done history of the company. Mike Longworth's *Martin & Co.: A History* (Four Maples Press) was first published in 1987. While there have been many subsequent books that cover the history of the company and its guitars, Longworth's efforts set a very high standard.

Gibson guitars are also very well documented. *Gibson Guitars: 100 Years of an American Icon* (General Publishing Group), edited by Walter Carter, was commissioned by the company itself. Even though it was produced by Gibson, it is a forthright account of the company and its instruments. A variety of authors have taken on specific aspects of Gibson history. *Gibson Electric* (Backbeat Books), also by Walter Carter, is a close look at the development of these instruments. *Gibson's Fabulous Flattops* (Backbeat Books), by Eldon Whitford et. al., as its title would suggest, looks at the flattop guitars made by the Gibson Company. It is a well written and well researched discussion of these wonderful instruments. *Gibson Guitars: Ted McCarty's Golden Era 1948 – 1966* (Hal Leonard) by Gil Hembree, looks at a specific period of Gibson guitar history that was remarkably innovative and productive. Lester Spann's *Guide to Gibson 1902-1941* (Centerstream) is an invaluable source for Gibson production totals and design features. It also looks at production and distribution systems. Andre Duchossoir's *Gibson's Electrics From the Origins Up To 1961*, was published in 1981. Many years later it remains an excellent source.

The guitars from Fender are also very well covered in literature. *The Fender Book* (Miller Freeman Books), by Tony Bacon and Paul Day, is a slim volume with beautiful illustrations of many standard and custom Fender instruments. *Fender: The Golden Age: 1946-1970* (Cassell Illustrated), by Martin Kelly, et al., is a fine book that examines the company from its beginning through its sale to CBS. There are several books written by participants in the Fender story. Bill *Carson's My Life and Times With Fender Musical Instruments* (Vintage Guitar

Books) is an interesting look behind the scenes of the California company by a man who was involved in the production of its instruments. He was also one of Leo Fender's "go to" guys when he needed to obtain a musician's opinion on guitars and amps. Fender, *The Inside Story* (Backbeat Books), by Forest White, is also interesting, although issues of personality clash tend to bubble up to the surface. Andre Duchossoir, *The Fender Stratocaster*, first published in 1987, and his companion book *The Fender Telecaster* (both by Hal Leonard), first published in 1991, are brief but important looks at those two iconic guitars. Jim Roberts, with perhaps a bit of hyperbole, wrote *How the Fender Bass Changed the World* (Backbeat Books). This informative book certainly shows that the Fender bass did indeed change the world for bass players.

Other guitar manufacturers are covered in additional books. Walter Carter's *The History of Ovation Guitars* (Hal Leonard) is a great look at this innovative company's products, goals, and production. *The PRS Guitar Book: A Complete History of Paul Reed Smith Guitars* (Backbeat Books), by Dave Burrell, is also a well-written, researched, and produced look at this important American company. *The Story of Paul Bigsby* (FG Publishing), by Andy Babick, is important because Paul Bigsby played such a significant, though often forgotten role, in the development of the modern solid body electric guitar. It too is well-written. There are several books about Gretsch, including *50 Years of Gretsch Electrics* (Backbeat Books), by Tony Bacon, and Jay Scott's *The Guitars of the Fred Gretsch Company* (Centerstream). Both are informative and entertaining. Richard R. Smith in his *Rickenbacker* (Centerstream) details the history of that company from 1931 until the book's publication date of 1987. Hans Moust's *The Guild Guitar Book* (Guitarchives) looks at that company's offerings from 1952 through 1977. Bob Carlin wrote *Regal Musical Instruments 1895 – 1955* (Centerstream). This book is an important look at what was once a very important American manufacturer. Similarly, Ron Rothman's *The Harmony Book* (Rothman's Department Store) takes another look at that very important American company. Jay Scott's slim book, *Kay Guitars* (Seventh String Press) is a beautifully illustrated volume that looks at that company's important contributions to American music making. *Neptune Bound: The Ultimate Danelectro Guide* (Centerstream), by Doug Tullock, is another loving look at a brand of instrument that performed an important role in bringing playable guitars to people at very reasonable prices. The company's innovation stands out.

There are some wonderful books that cover specific sorts of guitars or genres. *Cowboy Guitars* (Centerstream), by Steve Evans and Ron Middlebrook, is a detailed a look at these instruments. Special note should be made of Doug Green's *Singing in the Saddle* (Vanderbilt University Press and Country Music Foundation Press). Mr. Green, "Ranger Doug" of "Riders in the Sky," devoted twenty years to writing a complete history of the singing cowboy. His look at, and love for, that genre is evident in his work. The book is very well-written and readable. It is also extremely well-researched and illustrated. All in all, it is a beautiful book.

Richard Mark French, *Engineering the Guitar: Theory and Practice* (Springer Press) while not the only book that deals with the science and technology of guitar building, is one of the best. French is a teacher and researcher at Purdue University who also serves as a consultant for various guitar companies. Roger Siminoff's *The Luthier's Handbook: A Guide to Building Great Tone in Acoustic Stringed Instruments* (Hal Leonard) dissects the elements of design that Siminoff considers to have the most impact on the quality of sound.

In the area of general guitar books George Gruhn and Walter Carter's *Electric Guitars and Basses*, and *Acoustic Guitars and Other Fretted Instruments* (Miller-Freeman) are both entertaining, lavishly illustrated, and very well done in general. *Gruhn's Guide to Vintage Guitars*, (Backbeat Books) also by Gruhn and Carter, is an important resource. It is organized like a naturalist field guide, and aids in the identification of the various models of instruments. It is an invaluable source when trying to decode the intricacies of individual guitars.

Lest I forget, Tom Wheeler's *American Guitars* (Harper Perennial) was the first book to look at the great sweep of guitar history. It remains a valuable resource and must be acknowledged for its important place in the field.

This is just a brief survey of some of the sources that I've found helpful in researching the book you are holding today. It is by no means an exhaustive list, but will point you in the right direction for further reading.

Index

About the Author

Jay Pilzer is a retired history professor with a Ph.D. from Duke University. He is a long time guitar player and has written articles on guitars and the guitar industry for several guitar-oriented publications. Pilzer has been a guitar dealer for more than twenty years. He lives in Nashville.

Books Published by American History Press

(Visit www.Americanhistorypress.com for complete descriptions)

To order please call toll-free (888) 521-1789

1609: A Country That Was Never Lost – Kevin Wright. Perfect bound paperback $18.95

A Great Conveniency: A Maritime History of the Passaic River – Kevin Olsen. Perfect bound paperback $18.95

A Spirited War: George Washington and the Ghosts of the Revolution in Central New Jersey – Donald J. Peck. Perfect bound paperback $18.95

Children of the Cherokee East Volume One – Jeff Bowen. Perfect bound paperback $12.95

Complete Delaware Roll of 1898 – Jeff Bowen. Perfect bound paperback $12.95

Exploring the Mason Dixon Line – Jack Layton. Perfect bound paperback $17.95

From Georgia Tragedy to Oklahoma Frontier: A Biography of Creek Indian Chief Chilly McIntosh – Billie Jane McIntosh. Perfect bound paperback $18.95

Little Walkers Creek - A History of the Land and Its People – Rebecca Sox Sowers. Perfect bound paperback $24.95

Now We Are Enemies: The Story of Bunker Hill – Thomas Fleming - Special 50th anniversary edition hardback with decorated endpapers, a new Introduction by the author, and a Foreword by Edwin S. Grosvenor, Editor in Chief of *American Heritage* magazine. $22.95

Scottish Colonial Schemes 1620-1686 – George P. Insh. Perfect bound paperback $22.95

Simon Girty Turncoat Hero – Phillip Hoffman. Casebound hardcover/paperback $28.95/ $21.95

South Carolina 1775: A Crucible Year – Edmund Bator. Casebound hardcover $26.95

Souvenirs of the Past – William Lewis Bâby. Perfect bound paperback $18.95

Taking the High Ground: How Boston Broke the British Grip – Ted Clarke. Perfect bound paperback $14.95

The Story of Tecumseh – Norman S. Gurd. Perfect bound paperback $18.95

The Women of the American Revolution -Volumes I and II – Elizabeth Ellet. Perfect bound paperback $28.95

The Women of the American Revolution - Volume III – Elizabeth Ellet. Perfect bound paperback $22.95

Come Walk With Me: Exploring Fairview Park – Rockport Cemetery, Cuyahoga County, Ohio – Sharon Guinaugh. Perfect bound paperback, $24.95

Tomahawks and Treaties: Micajah Callaway and the Struggle for the Ohio River Valley – Rex Callaway. Perfect bound paperback, $22.95

The Story of Isaac Brock – Walter R. Nursey, Perfect bound paperback, - $18.95

Rocks, Riddles and Mysteries: Folk Art, Inscriptions and Other Stories in Stone – Edward J. Lenik - $18.95

A Knave Among Knights in Their Spitfires –Jerry Billing [former WW II Spitfire pilot]- $18.95

Ontario and the Detroit Frontier 1701-1814 – Hugh Cowan [reprint of classic history originally written in 1929]

Let Us Never Forget: Stories and Paintings of World War II – Francis J. MCGinley - $34.95

Kalamazoo Gals: A Story of Extraordinary Women & Gibson's 'Banner' Guitars of World War II –John Thomas $21.95

Akee Tree: A Descendant's Quest for His Slave Ancestors – Stephen Hanks – perfect bound paperback - $19.95

An American Journey of Hope: Perth Amboy, the Capital and Port City on Raritan Bay 1683-1790 – Donald Johnstone Peck – Casebound hardcover with dust jacket - $26.95

CPSIA information can be obtained at www.ICGtesting.com
Printed in the USA
LVOW11s2339271014

410753LV00004B/5/P